Trash or Treasure?

Edited by Andrea DiNoto and Cathy Cashion

A Tree Communications Edition
Published by Crown Publishers, Inc.

First printing: March, 1977. Printed and
bound in the United States of America.

ACKNOWLEDGEMENTS

The people who contributed time and knowledge to this book are too numerous to thank
individually. Collectors generously invited us
into their homes, often during scant free hours
in the evenings or on weekends, where they
showed, and allowed us to photograph, their
most treasured objects. Frequently, they gave
us the benefit of their own original research,
information not available in published sources.
Dealers, gallery owners, and auctioneers took
time from busy schedules to show us their
finest merchandise and to share the expertise
acquired over a lifetime.

Associate editors — Linda Campbell Franklin, William C. Ketchum, Jr., and Dennis
Southers — contributed much in the way of research and copy. Contributing photographer
John Garetti supplied us with many fine
photographs.

Several general references have proved in-
valuable. We are grateful for access, through
Linda Campbell Franklin, to her 11,000 title
bibliography on antiques and collectibles, to
be published in early 1978 by Scarecrow
Press, Metuchen, New Jersey. The Encyclopedia of Victoriana, edited by Harriet Bridgeman and Elizabeth Drury, New York, Macmillan Publishing Co., Inc., 1975, was constantly consulted. The Official Museum
Directory, published by the American
Association of Museums and National Register Publishing Company, Inc., 1975 made us
aware of many excellent public collections.

Our richest and most diverse resource, however, was New York City itself — its research
facilities, shops, galleries, and people — which
never ceases to educate and inspire those
fortunate enough to be here.

CREATED AND PRODUCED BY
Tree Communications, Inc.
250 Park Avenue South
New York, New York 10003

ASSISTING IN THE PRODUCTION OF THIS BOOK
Art Director: **Sonja Douglas**

Associate Designer: **Patricia Lee**

Photographer: **Steven Mays**

Production: **Lucille O'Brien**

COLOPHON
The text face for this book is Helvetica Light,
set at Examiner Graphics, Inc., and Tree
Communications, Inc. Halftones were made
by Tree Communications, Inc. The paper used
is Mall City Offset, made by Georgia Pacific
Corporation and supplied by Baldwin Paper
Company. The book was printed and bound
by R.R. Donnelley & Sons Co.

Di Noto, Andrea
    Trash or treasure?

    "A Tree Communications edition."
    1. Antiques.   I. Cashion, Catherine, joint
author.   II. Title.
NK1125.D444   745.1'075   76-53573
ISBN 0-517-52915-7

Contents

Introduction 4

Americana 6
Folk Art
Textiles
Navajo Blankets

Furnishings 17
Accessories
Furniture

Cupboard and Fancy Ware 24
Bottles and Jars
Pottery and Porcelain
Metalware
Glass

Useful Tools and Devices 50
Kitchen Utensils
Sewing Tools
Hand Tools

Packaging and Politics 66
Advertising Art
Trade Catalogs
Political Buttons

Getting Around 77
Bicycles
Automobiles
Railroadiana
Steamship Memorabilia

Posting a Message 89
Stamps and Covers
Postcards
Greeting Cards

Words and Images 100
Books
Posters
Prints
Maps
Photographica

The Entertainers 120
Theater
Dance
Movies
Phonographs
Records
Sheet Music

Playthings 138
Tin and Cast-Iron Toys
Banks
Parlor Games
Characters and Comics
Baseball Memorabilia
Dolls
Miniatures

Costumery 167
Clothing
Accessories
Jewelry
Buttons

Commemoratives and Currency 182
World's Fair Memorabilia
Coins

Collectors' Clubs and Periodicals 188

Introduction

It's a familiar dream, that of finding a treasure buried among a lifetime's worth of objects that have accumulated in attic, garage or basement. It usually begins on the day we decide to take stock, sorting through heirlooms, sentimental souvenirs, books, records, furniture, jewelry and clothing. While shaking the dust out of an old quilt or musing over an obsolete egg beater, we wonder, what's it all really worth, and what, if anything, should be thrown away? If you are the type who can't bear to part with things, you have the best chance of finding a treasure, not only among things of obviously good quality, but even in the debris of button boxes and burgeoning cartons that reside in life's dusty corners. It is a phenomenon of our times that many unexpected and intrinsically worthless objects are accorded unbelievable values by collectors. Collections as diverse as barbed wire and valentines hold rarities that bring high prices. Many are shown in the pages of this book. The discovery of a treasure leads inevitably to the question of what to do with it. One can display it with its newly acquired status (strongly recommended); make it the start of a collection; or attempt to sell it. Plunging into the world of collectors, dealers, and auctions is a sobering process, requiring steady nerves and a good deal of savvy if one is to emerge unscathed by the tricks of the trade. *The Insider's Guide to Antiques, Art and Collectibles* by Sylvia O'Neill Dorn is an excellent preparation and guide for the novice.

Pricing to Sell

It is a rule of thumb that the less you know of an item's current market value, the better chance a buyer has of making a profit at your expense. In general, when selling to a dealer, expect to receive, at most, 1/3 of the item's market value. Dealers' costs include overhead and, often, restoration and refurbishing of an item which is then marked up for resale and profit. The values given in this book were obtained from collectors, dealers, and auctioneers, and reflect 1976 estimated retail and auction prices for the specific objects shown. By consulting with several authorities in most cases, we have tried to arrive at an accurate estimate of each object's value at the time this book was printed. However, it should not be assumed that similar objects would bring the same evaluation in every case. The condition of an object has a direct effect on its value. Chips, dents, stains, and broken or replaced parts can make hundreds of dollars worth of difference. Also, prices change constantly, rising and falling with trends, from month to month, region to region, and shop to shop. A fashionable shop or boutique will necessarily charge more than an out-of-the-way dealer, even in the same town. You will also find opinions divided among dealers and collectors over the value of a particular object. So comparative personal research is essential when trying to establish a fair, accurate estimate. Appraisals for art, antiques, and collectibles should be sought only from reputable dealers, auctioneers, collectors and professional appraisers listed with established firms (such as the American Society of Appraisers in Washington, D.C.). In addition, one should insist on an appraiser who specializes in a particular field. Anyone who claims the ability to appraise a wide range of diverse objects is probably not reliable. Collectors often know the value of their objects with greatest accuracy, and selling directly to them is often the best course.

Advertising to Sell
The collectors' clubs and periodicals listed at the back of this book offer another market for selling your treasures. Most journals carry classified ads for merchandise wanted and for sale. Other more general collectors' publications in which one can advertise include the *Antique Trader*, *The American Collector*, *Collector's News* and *Hobbies Magazine*. All these and more are listed in *Ayers Directory of Publications*. Popular items such as Carnival Glass, postcards, bottles, and political items are regularly sold and traded at collectors' conventions. A collector with lots of money to spend will sometimes pay any amount to obtain a particularly rare and desirable object for his collection, especially if it is in mint condition. This is not the norm, however, and such prices are not true indicators of actual market values.

Auctions
Selling at auction represents a gamble. Prices realized on the auction block are not always predictable, nor do they necessarily reflect current market values. The exception to this is the fine arts market in which it is generally agreed that auctions do set values. You can keep abreast of auction prices by subscribing to auctioneers' catalogs and newsletters. One often hears a high price attributed to "auction fever," the result of spirited bidding by competing buyers who drive a price far beyond reasonable estimates. A seller may hope for, but should not expect, such luck. A poor turnout or a prevailing downbeat mood among buyers can reverse the process. Auctioneers offer the seller protection against unreasonably low bids through the reserve system, which establishes a minimum bid. In all auctions, the seller pays the auctioneer a commission, anywhere from 10% to 25%. Some houses establish the commission on a sliding scale according to the price realized.

Finder's Keepers
When the excitement of discovery subsides, the joy of possessing a treasure continues to come from showing it to and sharing it with others; not necessarily from selling it. Sharing sparks interest in a new subject and generates enthusiasm among others to enlist in the hunt. And the hunt can take you far afield, to fleamarkets, museums, libraries, and into fascinating areas of collecting you never knew existed. Whether your treasure turns out to be a toy, bottle, or rare first edition, once it is sold and converted to cold cash, it is gone forever. So consider the options seriously before giving up something unique and valuable. You may never find it again.

Americana

Vigor and inventiveness, words so often associated with the American character, are nowhere better expressed than in this country's folk art. Rooted in the craft tradition, its artists were common people with no formal training. Yet, the wealth of decorative and useful objects they created in the 18th and 19th centuries speak with a naive eloquence greatly admired by modern artists today. Those who recognized and appreciated this art, 30 or 40 years ago, are now reaping the rewards of foresighted collecting.

Folk Art: The Pennsylvania Dutch were masters of applied design, painting walls, floors and furniture with gay colors and patterns. They also decorated tinware, known as *tole*, with flowers, birds and animals. Prices for toleware in excellent condition begin in the high hundreds (p. 7). Their little chalkware figures, molded from plaster of Paris, were considered the poor man's Staffordshire. These household ornaments, often friendly-faced animals, were sold by itinerant peddlers for about 15 cents. Today, $1,800 would buy a choice piece (p. 7).

Weathervanes, astonishing in their variety, were produced in workshops and factories. Most were made of copper hammered over wooden forms. Few are one-of-a-kind. The prices range from the high hundreds to the high thousands of dollars; one pays for unusual designs and fine detailing on a rising scale (p. 8).

Wood-carvings reveal both a sense of whimsey and an innate understanding of form. Sculptors who set their hands to whirligigs and walking sticks (p. 11) also wrought trade signs (p. 10) and figureheads, butter molds and tobacconist figures. Cigar store Indians, as they were called, sold for $40 to $125 in the 1890s. Around 1910, a law banned them from sidewalks as pedestrian hazards – people would walk into them at night on unlit streets. This resulted in a "massacre" of the figures by store owners who sent them to junk yards. It is estimated, of the 75,000 figures that once existed, only 3,000 remain. In the late 1920s, you might have picked one up for $50; but today's Indians demand 100 times that ransom (p. 11).

Schoolgirls' theorem paintings on paper or velvet (p. 9) were once commonplace. Now,

they are considered critically, as any work of art, for composition, line and color.

Textiles: The womanly art of sewing was well-respected in early America. Intricately embroidered samplers produced by youthful hands are impressive displays of needlework that can bring over $100. The finest homespun quilts amaze us with their dazzling display of graphic designs, and prices range from the low hundreds to thousands of dollars for individual pieces.

Navajo Blankets: Like quilts, woven Navajo blankets are now considered less as craft and more as examples of pure design. Created with phenomenal intuitive skill by Navajo women, they are studied by artists and art historians alike. A first-phase Chief Pattern Blanket (1850-1860) once sold for $35,000. Two later styles shown on page 16 are more apt to be found tucked away in an attic trunk, but most have been collected. Examples occasionally come up for sale at auction.

Suggested Reading:
Bolton, Ethel Stanwood, and Eva J. Coe. *American Samplers*, Dover, 1973.
Christensen, E.O. *American Crafts and Folk Arts*, R.B. Luce, 1964.
Colby, Averil. *Samplers*, Branford, 1965.
Fitzgerald, Ken. *Weathervanes and Whirligigs*, Potter, 1967.
Holstein, Jonathan. *American Pieced Quilts*, Viking Press, 1973.
Kahlenberg, Mary, and Anthony Berlant. *The Navajo Blanket*, Praeger, 1972.
Ketchum, William C. *Hooked Rugs*, Harcourt Brace Jovanovich, 1976.
Kopp, Joel and Kate. *American Hooked and Sewn Rugs*, Dutton, 1975.
Lichten, Frances. *Folk Art of Rural Pennsylvania*, Scribner's, 1946.
Lipman, Jean, and Alice Winchester. *The Flowering of American Folk Art*, Viking, 1974.
Myers, Barbara. *Victorian Embroidery*, Nelson, 1963.
Stafford, Carleton, and Robert Bishop. *America's Quilts and Coverlets*, Dutton, 1972.

Folk Art

Tole Coffee Pot

During the 19th century, the Pennsylvania Dutch embellished many household objects with striking designs. Their quilts and painted furniture have long been regarded as prime examples of American folk art. Their painted tinware, known as *tole,* has only recently achieved a place of equal distinction. This 12-inch-high coffeepot has yellow, red, and green fruit and leaves painted on a black background. Less than five years ago, such pieces were easily bought for under $100. Today, pieces in excellent condition, like the one shown, can bring from **$1,800** to **$2,800**. *John Gordon Gallery, New York City.*

Nodding Chalkware Cat

Chalkware describes a type of hand-painted figurine made from molded plaster. Most of these 19th-century figures are animals less than 8 inches high. Because of their soft composition, they are difficult to find in good condition. This winsome cat is unusual on several counts: first, for its 10-inch size, second for its nodding-head construction, third for its mint condition, and, finally, for its winning colors — white with bright orange, yellow, and chocolate-brown markings. One could expect to pay at least **$1,800** for this rare kitty. *John Gordon Gallery, New York City.*

Cherub Weathervane

During the 19th century, American weathervanes were most often made of copper hammered over wooden forms. This method made it possible to produce many vanes from the same form. Vanes in the shapes of eagles and horses were most common. Angelic cherubs like the one above are rare. They were produced by several makers and boast excellent detail. This particular 28-inch vane still bears traces of the original gold leaf. Such weathervanes can bring up to **$3,800**, depending on condition.

Cow Weathervane

Not so rare as the cherub (above), this cow is of a typically New England design. Like the cherub, it shows good detail and a fine oxidized copper patina. Approximately 30 inches long, it is valued at about **$1,800**. *Photos this page courtesy of John Gordon Gallery, New York City.*

Theorem Painting

Theorem painting, along with needlecrafts and housework, was considered an acceptable homely pursuit for young women in the early 19th century. Basic outlines for still lifes — usually bowls of fruit or flowers — were stenciled onto paper or velvet, then tinted with oils or watercolors. In spite of the use of stencils, and although the quality of the tinting varies widely, great freedom of expression is often achieved. Theorems of exceptional quality can bring upwards of **$1,500**. *John Gordon Gallery, New York City.*

Half-Model

Building shadow box half-models was a 19th-century sailor's pastime. The worker carved half of a ship's hull, attached the sails and rigging to it, and then glued the construction into a shallow wooden box, fitted with a glass top. The "shadow box," as it was called, created an illusion of depth, particularly since its interior was painted to look like the sea and sky. Today, these half-models range in value from **$175** to **$300**, depending upon complexity.

Tramp Art

Itinerants, with plenty of spare time and a lot of imagination, fashioned unusual works from discarded objects they found in the streets. The elaborate faceting on this clock is made from cigar boxes. Tramp art, as it is called, is extremely valuable today. This clock goes for **$150**. *Courtesy of Helaine Fendelman, Scarsdale, N.Y.*

Decoy

Elmer A. Crowell, considered the best American decoy artist, carved and painted this flying mallard as an exhibition decoy about 1900. Although his works are not signed, serious collectors recognize his distinctive style immediately and are willing to pay **$3,000**, or more, for one such piece. *Courtesy of John Gordon Gallery, New York City.*

Bootmaker's Sign

Trade signs were often just a three-dimensional representation of the tradesman's specialty. Many items, like this wooden gilded boot, were hand carved in the 19th century with great care and skill, resulting in pieces more sculptural than commercial. While some may argue its merits as either advertising or folk art, collectors are likely to pay **$300** unquestioningly for such a find.

Whirligig

This 6-inch gentleman was a fearless pilot, or so his carver might have imagined. This whirligig was probably attached to a roof; the propeller showed the velocity of the wind, and the tail swung in the direction of the wind. This example of folk art is valued at **$350.** *Courtesy of Montgomery Ecklund Antiques, Stamford, New York.*

Walking Canes

The large wooden noses on these walking sticks make crazy but sturdy handles. The folk artist who carved them in the late 18th or early 19th century had either an imagination steeped in comical exaggeration or an obsession with noses. Today, the results of his inspiration are valued at **$75.** *Courtesy of Stonehouse Antiques, Lexington, New York.*

Indian Princess

The New York City sculptor Samuel Robb, working in the late 19th century, specialized in tobacconist and circus figures. This cigar-store princess, typical of his best work, is of carved and painted wood. In mint condition, with original paint, it stands 56 inches high (plus 24 inches for the base) and is valued at **$6,000.** Twenty years ago, such pieces might have been purchased for a few hundred dollars or less. *Photo courtesy of John Gordon Gallery, New York City.*

Textiles

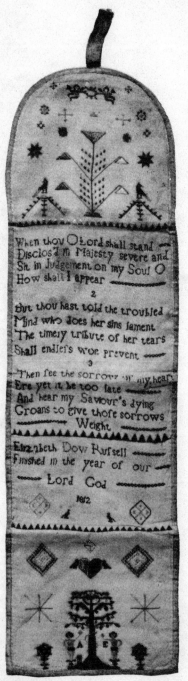

Wall Pocket

Elizabeth Dow Russell embroidered this wall pocket in 1812. Religious verses were considered the proper topics of young women's needlework. At the bottom, Miss Russell has stitched a humorous rendition of the Fall of Man. Her wall pocket is valued at **$250**. *All items pages 12-15 courtesy of Cora Ginsburg, Tarrytown, New York, unless otherwise indicated.*

American Sampler

This sampler by Susannah Murray contains an intricate floral border and sophisticated needlework images. The building is probably one located in her home town in Kentucky. The quality of the embroidery is even more remarkable when one realizes that Miss Murray was only eleven years old at the time she stitched the sampler. Her childhood artistry might be worth as much as **$350** now.

Bead-Work Souvenirs

American Indians made all sorts of beaded whimsies as souvenirs for the Victorian tourists who visited places like Niagara Falls. These stuffed boots, a matched pair, are unusually large (6 inches high) and more elaborately beaded than most. As a result, they are valued at approximately **$40.** *Courtesy of Norine Lewandowski, New York City.*

Mourning Sampler

This 1806 sampler, signed E.J., is a mourning piece, commemorating the tenth anniversary of the death of Sarah Wilkinson. It displays a picture and a variety of stitches, which contribute to its **$375** value.

Amish Quilt

The Amish people were known for their diamond patterns. The bold red and beige diamonds on a white background suggest this quilt to be of Amish origin. Though remarkably modern looking, this one dates from 1850, and is valued at **$475**.

Jacquard Coverlet

This coverlet from Pennsylvania was made on a loom with a Jacquard attachment. The attachment was invented in 1805 and made possible the repetition of a pattern weave by mechanical means. The new device also permitted more complicated patterns of three and four colors. This red, blue, yellow and green coverlet is valued at **$350.**

Rose of Sharon Quilt

The appliquéd foliage radiating from the center of this Pennsylvania Dutch quilt is an ornamental bush called the Rose of Sharon. It was a popular decorative motif in the 18th and 19th centuries. The birds at each corner are stuffed. The delicate stitching is what gives this quilt its **$1,300** value.

Quilt

This patterned quilt from Pennsylvania dates from 1850, and is valued at **$1,500**. Appliquéd, printed materials form the red and pink pinwheels and the green oak leaves. The carefully pieced border and the precise stitching contribute to the quilt's value.

Stevengraph

Signing of the Declaration of Independence.
JULY 4TH, 1776.

In 1870, Thomas Stevens of Coventry, England rescued the country's slumping textile industry with the creation of brilliantly colored silk ribbon pictures woven on the Jacquard loom. Intended as bookmarks, these instantly popular 3-by-5-inch novelties were sold by the thousands for 17 shillings. The most common subjects were hunting and racing scenes. This one of the signing of the Declaration of Independence, still in its original mounting, bears an authenticating label (below) on the back. In 1940, the bombing of Coventry destroyed thousands of Stevengraphs and the work cards necessary for weaving them. Today, those that remain are collectors' items at **$200-$300** apiece. *Courtesy of Sarah Potter Conover, Inc., New York City.*

Hooked Rug

Hooked rugs were a phenomenon of country living and were popular between 1840 and 1900. A hook was used to draw looped strips of cloth through a woven piece of background fabric. The strips were made from scraps or rags, which experienced a remarkable transformation in their new form. This 28-by-36-inch rug is worth **$300**.

Tape Rug

Tape rugs were made from rags cut into strips of tape which were sewn into a backing to form a lively and fluid design. Rags literally became riches. Today this rug, made in 1790, goes for **$750**.

Navajo Blankets

Eye Dazzler

From the late 18th to late 19th centuries, Navajo women produced blankets remarkable for the intricacy of the weaving and inventiveness of the design. Each was a unique creation, not based on patterns or drawings, but definite styles evolved in different periods. When aniline dyes became available to the Navajos in the 1880s, a wider selection of vivid colors appeared in their work. They found their most dramatic expression in the radiating diamond motif of the Eye Dazzler type blanket shown here. This blanket, 78 inches by 67 inches, is woven from handspun wool in black, orange, red-orange, yellow, and white. Blankets of this type, made from 1885 to 1890 have sold for as much as **$2,000.**

Late Serape Style

Today, collectors value Navajo blankets less as craft or apparel than as examples of abstract art. They are found in art museums and private collections around the world. This late serape style blanket, patterned with undulating serrated chevrons, was woven in the 1880s from aniline-dyed, four-ply wool in black, blue, red, and white. It measures 81 by 56 inches. Blankets of this type range in value from **$1,200** to **$3,500**. *These blankets from the collection of Anthony Berlant, Santa Monica, California. Photos courtesy of the Los Angeles County Museum of Art.*

Furnishings

It is the fortunate few who can regularly re-decorate their homes and apartments from top to bottom, changing styles with trends. While many decorate eclectically by choice, most are forced by circumstances to endure a comfortable hodge-podge of furnishings which they have either inherited or acquired at thrift shops and flea markets. But those who care about authenticity in general and antiques in particular, live with the constant hope that their Windsor chair is a real Windsor, not a reproduction; that their Victorian table was not made in Grand Rapids in the 1930s; and that their 19th-century schoolhouse clock has not, in fact, just rolled off the assembly line.

The satisfaction of knowing the true value of what we have paid for comes only with a great deal of study and often many disappointments. Expertise is hard won. Some people trust and buy only from established dealers, but this method is for those who can always afford to pay top dollar. Successful bargain hunters with limited means must be armed with first-hand knowledge of the marketplace, including dealers, auctions, private collectors, and even flea markets. They know there is no substitute for looking at, handling and, in general, becoming familiar with the feel of genuine articles.

An 18th-century American pipe box was auctioned recently for $1,900, paid for undoubtedly by a dealer or collector who recognized its unusual detailing and quality (p. 18). Still, $1,900 for such a crude, homely piece hardly seems possible. Yet, many humble-looking, country pieces are now among the highest priced furnishings around. For example, the smallest Shaker accessory, an oval storage box (p. 18), can bring over $500; an herb cupboard commands $4,000 (p. 20). Even a rustic, 18th-century Windsor chair for $750 is by no means the top of the line. These "stick" pieces were often made of elegant polished woods, and complete sets are rarities worth thousands today.

A re-evaluation of 19th-century furniture, from Empire to late Victorian, has placed a premium on items which were hard to give away as recently as 10 years ago. A Federal chest (p. 21) with original brasses could be a $1,200 discovery. Sleigh beds (p. 21), relegated to attics for years, are now in antique shops sporting price tags ranging from $600 to $800; even those typically "Renaissance Revival" Victorian chairs (p. 22), which dealers once left out in the rain to acquire a bit of aging, are bringing appreciative prices in the hundreds. Early 20th-century, mission-style, or craftsman, furniture (p. 23), particularly those pieces made by Stickley Brothers, are no longer gathering dust at the backs of shops. These sturdy, plain pieces are also the focus of a revival and may someday enjoy the prestige always accorded to Shaker pieces. Condition, original hardware, original paint or finish, and the area of the country in which it is sold drastically affect furniture prices. For example, pieces native to the East Coast, including both country and Victorian styles, could double in price in the West and Southeast.

Suggested Reading

Andrews, Edward Deming and Faith. *Religion in Wood: A Book of Shaker Furniture*. Indiana Univ. Press, 1966.

Bailey, Chris H. *200 Years of American Clocks and Watches*. Prentice-Hall, 1975.

Bridgeman, Harriet & Drury, Elizabeth. *The Encyclopedia of Victoriana*. Macmillan, 1975.

Comstock, Helen, ed. *The Concise Encyclopedia of American Antiques*. Hawthorn, 1965.

Davidson, Marshall B., ed. *The American Heritage History of American Antiques*. 3 volumes. American Heritage, 1967-69.

Kovel, Ralph and Terry. *American Country Furniture, 1780-1875*. Crown, 1965.

Lockewood, Luke. *Colonial Furniture in America, Volume 1 and 2*. Castle Books, 1926.

Nineteenth Century America, Furniture and Other Decorative Arts. Exhibition Catalogue. April 16-September 7, 1970, The Metropolitan Museum of Art, New York City.

Accessories

Shaker Boxes

The Shakers, in their elegant practicality, created oval wooden boxes in all sizes, for every storage need. Many are painted, and size is often designated by the number of "fingers" apparent on the side where the joint is made. Collectors like to acquire sets of graduated sizes. These sold at auction for **$310** (top) and **$575**.

18th-Century Spoon Rack

Like pipe boxes (right), spoon racks were usually crude household items bearing little or no embellishment. Any design, carving, or other detailing adds value to these artifacts of early-American life. This spoon rack's graceful, inverted heart motif, carved sides, and signs of wear, together with traces of the original red paint, contributed to its auction price of **$1,750**.

18th-Century Pipe Box

The pipe box shown here, about 18 inches high, held long-stemmed clay pipes in the top compartment and loose tobacco in the bottom drawer. Few have survived in good condition, and fewer still display such elaborate carving. Distinctly American, beautifully detailed with a double heart and crown crest, this one still shows traces of the original paint. It sold for **$1,900** at auction.

Eight-Day Weight Clock

An 1879 catalog lists this 32-inch-high Seth Thomas clock for $6.75. Today its grain-painted columns, porcelain face, and original decals set in a rosewood case could bring as much as **$450.** *Clock Hutt, Ltd., New York City.*

Schoolhouse Clock

A label, (shown at left) on the back of the 24-inch schoolhouse clock, identifies it as a "drop octagon," eight-day model made by the Waterbury (Connecticut) Clock Co. "Drop octagon" describes the shape of the clock and pendulum housing. Probably a $6-$7 original, one could expect to pay as much as **$400** for it today. *Clock Hutt, Ltd., New York City.*

No. 2 Regulator Weight Clock

Seth Thomas's weight-driven, regulator wall clocks were made during the late 19th century for use in schoolrooms and other public places. This 33-inch mahogany model, once modestly priced, is now in the **$600-$800** range. A 1976 reproduction offered for $360 has enhanced the value of the antique. *Clock above and right courtesy of Joseph Fanelli's Clocks and Things, N.Y.C.*

Repeating Carriage Clock

This 5-inch-high gilded-brass and crystal carriage clock is an hour repeater made in France for the New York firm of Tiffany and Co. at the turn of the century. It originally sold for under $50; **$650** would be a more likely estimate today, since hour repeaters of this type are rare.

Furniture

Herb Cupboard

Sturdy country furniture that offers lots of storage space has great practical as well as historic value. This large, yellow, painted Shaker cupboard once stored herbs in its numbered drawers. It sold at auction for **$4,250.**

Windsor "Bird Cage" Rocker

This rustic 18th-century rocker is so named for the curving, cagelike construction of the lower back sections, topped by a high comb. Windsors of this vintage are prized by collectors of American country furniture. This one might sell for about **$750.** *Courtesy of Ruggles House, Columbia Falls, Maine.*

Shaker Table

This simple, pine side table, by a Shaker cabinet maker, is respected by contemporary collectors for its simplicity and prophetically modern craftsmanship. It is valued at **$750**. *Courtesy of Ruggles House, Columbia Falls, Maine.*

Pilgrim Chest

When the Pilgrims came to America in the 1600s, they brought chests like this one with them. Made of heavy oak and standing 36 inches high, the chest is characterized by a massive shape and applied decorative spindles on front. Such a chest could bring as much as **$3,000.** *Courtesy of the Block House, Ellsworth, Maine.*

Federal Chest of Drawers

An expert would immediately assess this as a Federal period chest of drawers, noting the overall shape and construction, mahogany veneering, including that of the top drawer, which is carefully selected and matched, and the "demi-lune" crest. While most such chests are not marked, they are attributed to the New York cabinet maker, Michael Allison, who worked from 1800 to 1845. Solid, unveneered mahogany side panels, cut out at the bottom to form the feet, are a feature of such New York pieces, valued upwards of **$1,200** depending on condition. The original hardware, as this one has, increases value.

Sleigh Bed

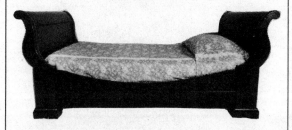

Named for their sleighlike curved ends, these beds were an expression of the Empire style produced in America about 1850. Thirty years ago, people found them difficult to give away, owing perhaps to the new popularity of larger, more streamlined beds. Today, a mahogany example like this could bring from **$600** to **$800** depending upon condition.

Empire Dressing Table

The formality and elegance of the Empire style is evident in this early-19th-century table. Resplendent with swanlike mirror supports, turned columns and feet, and ormolu mounts and drawer pulls, it also boasts a thick platform of richly figured mahogany veneer. The mirror, or petticoat glass, at the rear of the platform helped ladies of the period to check the length of their gowns. The platforms usually cracked with age; such cracks are considered a sign of authenticity today. Long out of vogue, such tables are a lucky find today for under **$800**. *All furniture pages 21 and 22 courtesy of Mary Heming Antiques, New York City.*

Gentleman's Chair

"Renaissance Revival" describes the style of this Victorian armchair from the 1870s. Of American manufacture, it was a popular style in its time and was made in all price ranges. Characterized by areas of raised burl veneers and carved and applied ornament, such chairs were long considered unfashionable and thus purchasable at $20-$30. Today **$150-$250,** depending upon condition, would be a modest estimate.

Ebonized Slipper Chair

Oriental influence on American styles gave rise to a vogue for ebonized furniture in the 1880s. The smooth, black ebonized finish was created by applying black shellac or lacquer to a close-grained wood — usually cherry. This chair's machine-turned spindles and incised wood detailing are characteristic of the Eastlake style. Resurging interest in such pieces places its value in the **$200** to **$300** range.

Gothic Dining Chair

Chairs of this type were made in America during the 1830s and '40s. This particular chair of mahogany, with vase-shaped center splat and mahogany veneering, exhibits untypical Gothic carving in the crest. Such chairs were usually made in sets of six that included one arm chair. Anything under **$100** for one such chair — considering its fine condition and the richness of the wood — would be a bargain. A complete set might be found for **$400** to **$500.**

Herter Library Table

Herter Brothers was established in the 1880s as one of the first interior decorating firms. They also designed and manufactured furniture. Many of their pieces of this period bear the distinctive golden marquetry of stylized chrysanthemums evident in this ebonized 44-by-30-inch-high library table made of exotic woods and veneers. Herter pieces are in the collection of several museums, including the Metropolitan Museum of Art in New York City. Depending on condition, pieces signed "Herter Bro's." could be worth thousands. *Courtesy of Mary Heming Antiques, New York City.*

Wooten Patent Secretary

Wooten desks, with their complicated system of cubbyholes and slots, were a typical Victorian phenomenon. Long considered more as oddities than serious antiques, they now command serious prices, attesting perhaps to the enduring charm of having everything at arm's length. This one sold at auction for **$3,000.**

Craftsman Furniture

A type of spare, functional, durable furniture was made from 1898 to the first decade of the 20th century in a reaction to ornate Victorian styles. Derived from the English Arts & Crafts movement, its designers, who included architects, utilized native American woods and revealed construction (in which construction details are apparent). Many well-crafted pieces were made by the Stickley Brothers, leaders of this American design movement; and any piece bearing this name increases its value. This cabinet, though unsigned, now brings about **$200**. *Courtesy of Mary Heming Antiques, New York City.*

Cupboard and Fancy Ware

The everyday things that fill the cupboards and shelves of the average household are valued mostly for their utility and decorative qualities. Stacks of dishes, glassware, pots, and pans usually add up to a fairly commonplace and predictable assortment. But the back of the closet sometimes yields a treasure in the form of an unexpected antique or odd collectible.

Bottles and Jars: Bottles and jars are the focus of hordes of serious collectors whose hobby is now ranked with stamp and coin collecting as the most popular in the United States. Antique bottles and flasks, as one would expect, can bring great rewards; but even veteran collectors blinked in amazement when single bottles went for five-figure sums at a recent auction (opposite). These are records that may never be broken, but valuable antique bottles and jars (p. 28) are still available to those who can recognize rare colors, unusual shapes and labels. The collecting of modern bottles is also a serious business. Several well-known liquor companies, following the lead of the James B. Beam Distilling Company, have been bottling their spirits for years in figural ceramic containers. The resultant craze for these bottles has produced some modern rarities with intriguing names like "First National Bank of Chicago" and "Agnew Elephant," (p. 27).

Pottery and Porcelain: Rustic, hand-formed American pottery is popular now as more and more people begin to understand and appreciate the rare 18th- and 19th-century types. Redware and salt-glazed stoneware (p. 36) are often considered an important area of folk art if the decoration is unusual. But the 19th century also produced novelties that are valuable today. "Old Sleepy Eye" pottery (p. 37) was once given away in flour sacks, and Occupational Shaving Mugs that dressed the shelves of local barber shops can bring from $150 to $250 (p. 37). The more recent pieces you might find gathering dust on a top shelf are a Fiesta Ware cookie jar or grandma's Roseville teapot (p. 35). If grandma was fond of oriental patterns, the teapot might be a valuable piece of Chinese Export porcelain (p. 31). Decorative limited-edition plates produced by several porcelain companies are collected and traded like stocks these days. The first of these plates is now a $3,000 collector's item (p. 33).

Glass: Tiffany lamps and art glass were found in many American homes in the early decades of this century. Many people now bemoan their lack of foresight in letting them slip through their fingers. An inexpensive Tiffany lamp is now $1,000 (p. 42). A Quezal art-glass vase brings over $4,000 (p. 44). But even more amazing is the fact that single pieces of Carnival Glass, the cheaply produced Tiffany imitation, also bring thousands of dollars at auction from serious collectors who have cataloged the rare colors and patterns. Depression Glass has its own chic, too. Particular patterns and colors are fast rising in the ranks of desirability (p. 48).

Metalware: Antique pewter, copper, and even early silver plate can also have value. The expert distinguishes the true antique from the modern reproduction by marks the old pewter- and silversmiths applied to their pieces (p. 38). Knowing the shapes that characterized a particular period helps to identify a 17th-century candlestick (p. 40), for example, or a pair of Federal-period andirons (p. 41).

Suggested Reading

Ebert, Katherine. *Collecting American Pewter.* Scribner, 1973.

Ketchum, William C. *Pottery & Porcelain Collector's Handbook.* Funk & Wagnalls, 1971.

Ketchum, William C. *A Treasury of American Bottles.* Bobbs-Merrill, 1975.

Kovel, Ralph and Terry. *Dictionary of Marks – Pottery and Porcelain.* Crown, 1953.

McKearin, Helen and George S. *American Glass.* Crown, 1941.

Rust, Gordon A. *Collector's Guide to Antique Porcelain.* Viking Press, 1973.

Weatherman, Hazel Marie. *Colored Glassware of the Depression Era, Books 1 and 2. Privately published, 1972.*

Bottles and Jars

Jared Spencer Flask

Possibly the most famous bottle sale of the century occurred in 1975, when this Early American pressed-glass pint flask was auctioned from the Charles B. Gardner Collection for **$26,000**. "Jared Spencer" and "Manchester Con" appear on the round medallion above the diamond-quilted patterning. It is olive-amber in color, and has a sheared mouth and a scarred base. *Photo courtesy of Robert W. Skinner, Inc., Bolton, Mass.*

Lady's Leg Bitters Bottle

Collectors will go to any length to complete a set. A winning bid of **$7,000** in 1975 bought this bottle marked "Phd and Co" and "Sazarac Aromatic Bitters," dating from around 1880. At the same auction, a similar bottle in milk glass brought only **$325**. But this ¾-quart size in deep cobalt blue was the rarity someone was waiting for.

18th-Century Seal Bottle

This long-necked, bulbous bottle dates from 1750. The applied-initial seal indicates that it was a customized container for a gentleman's spirits. The seal and the age of this unearthed bottle make it a **$500** rarity. *Courtesy of Jim's Bottle Shop, Ardsley, New York.*

Sunburst Flask

This aqua flask is decorated with an abstract embossed figure called the sunburst. The sunburst flask appeared in the first half of the 19th century, one of the earliest of figured flasks. The design was meant to attract a customer's eye to the bottle's alcoholic contents. Some 30 different examples of sunburst flasks are known; this one is valued at **$300**.

Bitters Bottle

Bitters were a unique form of medicine, dear to the hearts of men whose spouses had joined the Temperance Union. The shapes and colors of the bottles were as varied and interesting as the percentage of alcohol in their contents. This is the only known example of a labelled Congress Bitters bottle, and is valued at **$450**. *Courtesy of Jim's Bottle Shop, Ardsley, New York.*

Candy Jar

Candy bottles molded in the form of cars, rolling pins and other common objects were popular with both children and adults. Twentieth-century clear-glass containers are common enough, but colored-glass candy jars, like this 5-inch, red glass lantern with gold trim, are rare. This lantern goes for **$35**. *Courtesy of Jim's Bottle Shop, Ardsley, New York.*

First National Bank of Chicago

There are over 12,000 members of Beam Bottle Collectors' Clubs in the United States and abroad. They are a testimonial to the popularity of the figural liquor bottles designed and manufactured by the James Beam Distilling Company since the 1950s. Millions of dollars change hands at annual Beam bottle conventions where collectors seek and find the rarities. The most valuable Beam bottle is this **$3,000** "First National Bank of Chicago," produced in 1964 to commemorate the bank's 100th anniversary. The bottle is blue and gold and stands 11½ inches high. Of the 128 bottles made to commemorate the event, 117 were given to the directors of the bank. *Photo courtesy of Fred's Bottles, Cheyenne, Wyoming.*

Schiaparelli Perfume Bottle

Perfume bottles are a sub-specialty in the world of bottle collecting. In the 1940s, this flame-stoppered Schiaparelli candle flacon held the designer's special scent, "Sleeping." Touches of red and gold add to its **$25** value. *Courtesy of Harriet Love, New York City.*

Agnew Elephant

Running a close second to the rare "First National Bank of Chicago" is this Republican elephant made to honor former Vice-President Spiro Agnew at a $100-a-plate fund-raising dinner on November 12, 1970. The elephant forms the bottle's stopper. Beam bottle collectors waited outside for the elephant-bearing guests to emerge and offered $100 for one of the 196 bottles distributed at the dinner. Now, there are standing offers of **$2,400** for an Agnew Elephant, filled or empty. *Photo courtesy of the James B. Beam Distilling Co., Chicago, Illinois.*

Poison Bottle

If the word poison, broadly embossed on this miniature, cobalt-blue bottle, does not keep the foolhardy away, the leering skull certainly will. The small size of this 3-inch-high poison bottle increases its value to **$350**. *Courtesy of Jim's Bottle Shop, Ardsley, New York.*

Quart Fruit Jars

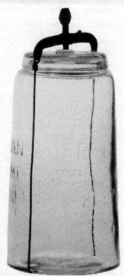

Very few jars have wires running completely around the jar. Two are shown here: The one on the left, embossed "Gilberds Improved Jar," was made in aqua and green around 1885. It is handmade with a ground lip and worth about **$125**. On the right is the famous Van Vliet, marked "Van Vliet Improved Pat'd May 3 81." The jar is colorless, has a ground lip, and was probably made in Pennsylvania. It is valued at about **$300**. *From the Alex Kerr Collection. Photo by Norris McCay.*

The Ne Plus Ultra

This green fruit jar tells its own tale: "The Ne Plus Ultra Airtight Fruit Jar Made By Bodine & Bros. W'mstown, N.J. For Their Patent Glass Lid." The lid says, "Ludlow's Patent August 6 1861 and June 28 1859." It is handmade with a ground lip. The color, the abundant embossing, and the scarcity of this jar all contribute to its value which is about **$1,000**. This one lacks the metal cage which held the lid. *From the Alex Kerr Collection. Photo by Norris McCoy.*

Pottery and Porcelain

Yorkshire Pottery

The rustic quality of this gentle, dock-tailed horse appeals as much today as in 18th-century England where such figurines with a sporting motif were especially popular. Made of Yorkshire pottery, it is a **$1,600**, 7-inch beauty. *Courtesy of Price Glover, Inc., New York City.*

Staffordshire Figurines

Rustic Staffordshire miniatures decorated Victorian shelves both in England and America. Tiny, hand-painted animals were among the most popular subjects. The earlier pieces are the most valuable. Today this 3-inch-high sheep and 2-inch-high cat, both from the 1820s, are valued at about **$200** each. The 2¼-inch rabbit, dating from 1840, is worth about **$125**. *Courtesy of Sarah Potter Conover, Inc., New York City.*

Posset Pot

The common cold in 18th-century England found a tough adversary in the remedy that filled this pot—posset, or hot milk mixed with wine or ale. The pot was carried to the invalid, who sucked the invigorating brew from the spout. Made of English delft, this lovely healer will present you with a **$900** doctor's bill. *Courtesy of Price Glover, Inc., New York City.*

Toby Mug

Shakespeare's carousing character, Sir Toby Belch, might have inspired this 9½-inch Staffordshire mug made by the prestigious Ralph Wood factory of Burslem, England, in 1765. Toby Mugs come in a variety of figures, including one woman, but the one shown here is the standard form. A very popular item among collectors, this mug sells for nearly **$1,000**. *Courtesy of Leo Kaplan Antiques, New York City.*

Stirrup Cup

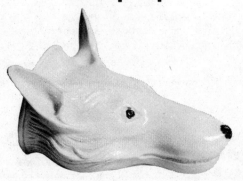

In 18th-century England, hunters mounted on horseback would quaff a farewell drink from this stirrup cup, handed up by well-wishers (with the dog's nose pointing downward). Made of Leeds pottery, this relic of the chase is worth **$500** today. *Courtesy of Price Glover, Inc., New York City.*

Nanking Soup Tureen

The spearhead border around the lid of this Chinese Export soup tureen identifies it as Nanking ware. Traces of gold on the finial and handles, and the overall fine quality of the blue-white underglaze decoration, date its manufacture around 1820. Later-made pieces are often identified by a cruder rendering of the applied design. In perfect condition, Nanking tureens are worth as much as **$1,200**. *All items this page courtesy of Sarah Potter Conover, Inc., New York City*.

Chinese Export Teapot

The shape of a China trade teapot is often a clue to when it was made; many imitate popular European shapes. This one, with an uncommon scene of goats and a goatherd, stands 8 inches high and features an unusual handle with a bamboo motif. It dates from the 1820s and would sell for **$400-$500**.

Canton Hot-Water Plate

The familiar river and temple scene that inspired English willowware is evident on this octagonal hot-water dish. The scalloped inner border identifies it as valuable Canton ware, and the fine quality of the hand-painted design dates it from the 1820s. It measures 9½ inches in diameter and is estimated at **$375**.

Elephant Candlesticks

This is one of a pair of very rare Chinese Export candlesticks made around 1820. Candlesticks like this were made in different colors. These are orange and measure 10 inches by 8 inches. Their mantles are decorated in a pattern similar to the rose mediallion motif. A pair in excellent condition has sold for as much as **$4,500**. *Photos above and at right courtesy of Sarah Potter Conover, Inc., New York City.*

Nanking Tea Caddy

A spearhead border, characteristic of Nanking ware, graces the shoulders of this porcelain tea caddy. Once part of a set, it originally had a china stopper and held tea leaves. Possibly made in the 18th century, it is valued at **$225**.

Serving Bowl

This serving bowl, dated 1910, was an early example of the Art Deco style which was to become popular after World War I. Probably made by Gustav Gurschner, the 10-inch-high ceramic piece is valued today at **$350**, even though it is unsigned. *Courtesy of Robert K. Brown.*

First Bing and Grondahl Plate

In 1895, Bing and Grondahl of Copenhagen, created 500 of these blue and white porcelain plates as a Christmas novelty. They sold for approximately 75 cents and were intended to replace plain, wooden plates Danes traditionally filled with sweets for gift-giving. The idea caught on immediately and launched the limited-edition, collectors' plate "industry." Today this plate is worth more than **$3,000**, according to the Bradford Exchange of Chicago, a firm which tabulates bi-monthly price quotations on all collectors' plates based on actual items sold and traded. *Photo courtesy of Bing and Grondahl.*

Viennese Vase

The most prestigious workshop of the applied arts in early-20th-century Vienna was the Wiener Werkstaette. The innovative group inspired many other artists to form similar guilds. This 12-inch ceramic vase was made in 1912 by Michael Powolny, a founder of the Wiener Keramik group. The vase is valued at **$500**. *Courtesy of Robert K. Brown.*

Christmas Plate

In 1908, the Danish porcelain manufacturer Royal Copenhagen issued its first Christmas plate, "Maria with Child," to compete with a rival company, Bing and Grondahl. It is not known how many plates were made, but they were originally priced at 75¢. Today this plate is valued at over **$1,000**. All porcelain Royal Copenhagen plates are blue and white. This first Christmas plate measures 6 inches in diameter; succeeding issues are 7¼ inches. Plates made from 1940-1946 are valued at well over **$100** each. *Photo courtesy of The Royal Copenhagen Porcelain Manufactory, Ltd., Denmark.*

Hummel Figure

Beginning in 1935, the drawings of Sister Maria Innocentia Hummel, a member of the Franciscan order from 1927 until her death in 1946, were transformed by Germany's W. Goebel factory into the popular figurines known as Hummels. Sister Hummel's Seissen Convent, near Saulgau, Germany, still receives a royalty on every Hummel figurine produced by Goebel. Plump-cheeked children are the Hummel trademark, but there are many other ceramic designs. This "Madonna with the Blue Cloak," marked and numbered 151, is one of Goebel's most valuable Hummels. Made for a brief period in the 1950s, it is a rarity today and sells for **$2,500**. *All items this page from the collection of Robert L. Miller.*

Auf Wiedersehen

A Hummel figurine very similar to this one, also called *Auf Wiedersehen*, is still manufactured by W. Goebels today and sells for $39 in retail stores. But the 1950s version pictured here has two significant details which distinguish it from the contemporary counterpart: the little boy wears a Tyrolean hat and holds no handkerchief. These two details define a rarity for which collectors will pay **$1,500**.

Swaying Lullaby

The banner beneath this sleeping child reads "Dreaming of Better Times," an expression of German hopes after World War II. Collectors feel certain that this 4-by-5-inch plaque, called *Swaying Lullaby*, was never sold in the United States, for no record of it has been uncovered in trade catalogs. As a result, it is a difficult item to find in America now and costs up to **$1,200**.

Fiesta Cookie Jar

If cookie jars had self-images, this one would certainly be proud. Following the dictates of the American dream, this container—with an uncommon Fiesta decal pattern—has steadily bettered itself since 1936. Originally sold at low prices in hardware and dime stores, it is now sought after by collectors who will gladly part with **$75** to share its company. *Courtesy of As Time Goes By, New York City.*

Fiesta Candlesticks

These tripodal candleholders, in the inverted ziggurat, which is an Art Deco trademark, are interesting examples of Fiesta Ware, and avidly sought even at **$75** a pair. *Courtesy of As Time Goes By, New York City.*

Roseville Teapot

In 1892, George Young of Zanesville, Ohio, started Roseville Pottery, a leader in American art pottery. His pottery graced American tables until 1954. This soft pink teapot with white flowers and green leaves, probably manufactured in the 1940s, is worth **$40**. *Photo courtesy of Non Sequitur, New York City.*

Redware Dish

Redware is a type of l9th-century American pottery named for the reddish-brown clay from which it was made. Decorative elements, such as wavy lines and flourishes, were often applied with yellow slip, a type of glaze that gives this pottery its other name—slipware. Much redware was made for everyday use in the form of pitchers, platters, and bowls, but few pieces are personalized like this one. "Mary's Dish" is 11 inches in diameter and conservatively valued at **$1,200**. *Courtesy of John Gordon Gallery, New York City.*

Bennington Crock

Until 1896, Bennington, Vermont was the production site of America's most famous folk pottery. Any marked Bennington piece is valuable. The swirling cobalt-blue floral decoration on this stoneware crock is unusually elaborate, and increases its worth to **$500**. *Courtesy of Fran Faulkner, New Kingston, New York.*

Stoneware Pitcher

This 9-inch-high stoneware pitcher boldly satirizes the political figures of the 1880s. One thin lackey dutifully strains to be a handle; the three portly bosses are sneering. It is not known which citizen from Anna, Illinois, exercised his First Amendment freedom, but his political wit is a **$300** treasure now. *Courtesy of Illinois State Museum, Springfield, Illinois.*

Old Sleepy Eye

"Old Sleepy Eye" is the name of the cobalt-blue Indian silhouette which decorates this 10-inch-high stoneware pitcher. During the early 20th century, he was the advertising emblem for a midwestern flour and coffee distributor. Any piece of stoneware bearing this image is highly collectible. This one is worth **$70**. *Courtesy of Illinois State Museum, Springfield, Illinois.*

Early 19th-Century Stoneware Jug

Stoneware is an extremely hard pottery made for utilitarian purposes. The incised fish on this 14-inch American jug is unusual, for most stoneware of this period was plain. Those decorated with lions, birds, fish and flowers are quite valuable today. This one goes for **$450**.

Occupational Shaving Mugs

Barbers once publicized their services by supplying customers with personalized shaving mugs. White porcelain blanks were hand painted to order with an illustration of a man's occupation and often his name. The mug was displayed at the barber shop, ready for the customer's use. Mugs showing trades or occupations like bartenders and carpenters are common; professions or unusual occupations are rare. Mugs range in value from **$150-$250** or more, depending upon the quality of the artwork.

Metalware

American Pewter Porringer

A porringer was a standard item in every American household during the nation's early years. Those made by Samuel Hamlin of Providence, Rhode Island, a prestigious and very prolific smith, are still available, and if in good condition, like the one shown here, may bring **$1,000**. *All items pages 38 and 39 courtesy of Price Glover, Inc., New York City.*

Pewter Teapots

These two pewter teapots may look about the same to the untrained eye, but an expert would spot the treasure. In 1770, pewtersmith Elizabeth Scott of Exeter, England, put her mark on the shapely teapot on the left, which now sells for over **$1,000**. The pewter teapot on the right from 1820 has less than 20 percent of the worth of its near-contemporary, still no mean sum.

Irish Haystack Measures

These Irish Haystack measures made of pewter by Austen & Sons, Cork, Ireland, could be found in all the local pubs in the 1820s. Government officials made periodic checks of each pub's set of measures to verify the proprietor's honesty in serving a proper half-pint, pint, or noggin, the three volumes shown above from left to right. The inspectors' excise marks can be seen on the inside lips of the measures. A full set of seven would include four other officially recognized measures—quart, half-gallon, gallon, and the smallest, half-noggin. Individual measures would be worth **$125-150** a piece today, but a complete set would be worth considerably more than the sum of its parts.

Britannia Coffee Pot

In the 19th century, tin, copper, and antimony were combined with pewter to form a new metal rolled in sheets, called Britannia. Wares like this coffee pot were formed from these sheets instead of molded like traditional pewter. The gracefully carved wooden handle contributes to this pot's **$125** value.

Queen Anne Commemorative Spoon

The relief-cast portrait of Queen Anne on the handle of this pewter spoon does not mean it was part of the royal family's flatware. Rather, it was produced cheaply for use at banquets and celebrations throughout England on Queen Anne's coronation day in 1702. Thousands were made, yet today they are valued at **$200** each. Most of the English monarchs after 1688 are represented on similar commemorative ware.

Brass Candlestick

Copper Kettle

Kettles, handmade of sheet copper about 1840, were indispensable hearth utensils. This one, obviously in good condition, measures 12 inches high by 9 inches wide and could sell for **$75** to **$100**; more if it had a gooseneck spout. *Courtesy of Ruggles House, Columbia Falls, Maine.*

Brass candlesticks cast in this tiered design were particularly popular in England during the Cromwellian period, 1650-1660. Many were imported by the American colonies for household use. Although brass, a base metal, this candlestick, discovered in an excavation, is worth **$850**. *Courtesy of Price Glover, Inc., New York City.*

Tankard

This pewter tankard, made late in the reign of Charles II (1660-1685), was later hand decorated with a portrait of William and Mary to commemorate their coronation. The tankard has a flat lid and a ram's horn thumbpiece; the mark of the maker contributes to its **$4,000** value. *Courtesy of Price Glover, Inc., New York City.*

Art Nouveau Candelabrum

Imagine discovering this fine, 21-inch-high silver-plated candelabrum painted white! The perpetrator of the crime appreciated neither its excellent Art Nouveau design nor the authenticating mark, "Barbour Silver Co.," a forerunner of International Silver, which dates the piece from around 1901. Such a piece might bring **$800** today. *Courtesy of Mary Heming Antiques, New York City.*

Federal Andirons

The bulbous turnings on these hollow-cast brass andirons suggest the Federal style popular around 1800. Once commonplace on every hearth, andirons like these are now worth as much as **$300**. *Courtesy of Axtell Antiques, Deposit, N.Y.*

Brass Tray

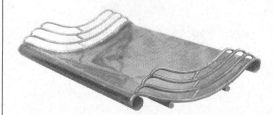

Joseph Hoffman, one of the founders and a continuous mentor of the Wiener Werkstaette, was an architect, professor, and leading designer in the early 20th century. This brass tray, dated 1915, is one of his creations. Its curving lines reflect the more fluid, less geometric shapes of the later Wiener Werkstaette. Measuring approximately 13 inches by 8 inches by 2 inches, the tray is valued at **$650** because it bears Hoffman's signature. *Courtesy of Robert K. Brown.*

Glass

Three-Lily Tiffany Lamp

Only 15 inches high, this signed Dore Tiffany lamp has three gold glass lily shades, also signed. Considering the five-figure prices elaborately leaded glass Tiffanys usually command, this one was a bargain, auctioned recently for **$1,050**. *Photos this page courtesy of Frank Roan III, McEwensville, Pennsylvania.*

Durand Frog

This whimsical blue frog supporting a yellow water lily is probably one of six such pieces made by the Frenchman Victor Durand, who established the famous Vineland Flint Glass Works in New Jersey in 1897. A special department within the factory began producing art glass in 1924. The 10-inch piece of Durand art glass sold at auction for **$1,550**.

Amberina Stork Vase

Amberina is a type of Victorian art glass characterized by red-to-gold color gradation. This 4-inch-high stork vase is a rare piece of pressed Amberina glassware made in limited number by the New England Glass Company in 1884. The few examples known to exist in private collections are valued at **$500** to **$600**.

Royal Flemish Vase

The Mt. Washington Glass Company advertised itself as "Headquarters in America for Art Glass Wares," because the company was always developing new types of decorated wares. Royal Flemish, a colored satin glass decorated with raised gilt designs, was developed in 1889. Oriental motifs inspired the form and patterning of this Royal Flemish vase. It was auctioned in March, 1976, for **$1,200**. *Courtesy of Patrick R. Welsh, auctioneer, New Boston, New Hampshire.*

Burmese Toothpick Holder

In 1885, the Mt. Washington Glass Company of New Bedford, Massachusetts, produced a new type of opaque art glass shaded from yellow to pink. Called Burmese ware, it was made by fusing glass with oxides of uranium and gold. To publicize their accomplishment, the company presented Queen Victoria with a set of Burmese glassware decorated with a floral pattern. Thomas Webb, the innovative British art-glass producer, manufactured the glass in England and renamed it Queen's Burmese. This 3-inch Queen's toothpick holder, made by Thomas Webb & Sons, sold at auction in September, 1976, for **$150**. *Courtesy of Patrick R. Welsh, auctioneer, New Boston, New Hampshire.*

Gallé Vase

The unique, colorful creations of Emile Gallé of Nancy, France, were exhibited in Paris in 1878 and 1889. They were part of the development of Art Nouveau glass at the end of the 19th century and inspired some of Tiffany's work. This signed, 20-inch Gallé vase is ribbed-shaped, colored brown, pink, and green and brought **$2,500** at auction. *Photo courtesy of Frank Roan III, McEwensville, Pennsylvania.*

Quezal Jack in the Pulpit

This classic Art Nouveau shape was originated by Tiffany, but a Brooklyn firm called Quezal, after the iridescently colored national bird of Guatemala, executed this imitation designed by Martin Back. One of the earliest glasswares to borrow Tiffany's ideas, Quezal is now collected in its own right. This 12-inch vase, in amber and gold iridescent shades, sold for **$4,500** at auction in 1976. *Photo courtesy of Frank Roan III, McEwensville, Pennsylvania.*

Wheeling Peachblow Condiment Set

Wheeling, West Virginia, was the home of the noted American glass works Hobbs, Brockunier & Company. Their peachblow ware graced many Victorian tables in the 1880s. Named for its soft, peach-to-rose shadings, peachblow took many forms. The mint condition of this condiment set brought **$325** at auction.

Lalique Plate

Lalique, a famous name in French art glass, created a limited-edition, crystal plate for the first time in 1965. The 2,000 made were instantly absorbed by enthusiastic plate collectors around the world at the original issue price of $25. The "Two Birds" plate is now worth at least **$1,000**. *Photo courtesy of Jaques Jugeat.*

Goblet

Josef Hoffmann was one of the founders of the Wiener Werkstaette, a group of artists who made highly sophisticated, decorative, but functional objects in Vienna during the early 20th century. This goblet, designed by Hoffmann in 1916, was painted with an oriental motif by Dagobert Peche, another member of the innovative group. The glass is marked with a WW monogram. Today, such pieces bring as much as **$600**. *Courtesy of Robert K. Brown.*

Cut Glass

Deep cutting and elaborate patterning is typical of late 19th-century cut glass, shown here. This hand-cut glass is often confused with the less expensive pressed glass, made in molds with traditional cut-glass patterns. The difference lies in the sharpness of the edges of cut glass, as well as in the price tags. The carafe, celery dish, and bowl pictured here range from **$100** to **$350** apiece in value. *Courtesy of Wood Shed Antiques, Machias, Maine.*

Lightning Rod Ball

From about 1860 to the early 1900s, colorful glass globes were used to decorate lightning rods. Most often found atop Midwest farmsteads, they range from common, plain white milk glass to this very rare, orange milk glass ball with star design. One of two known to exist in private collections, it is valued at **$1,500**. *From the collection of Ben Foley. Photo by Norris McCoy.*

"Lafayet" Salt

The Boston and Sandwich Glass Company of Sandwich, Massachusetts, made this 3½-inch-long open salt container in the style of local paddle wheel vessels. The ship's stern reads "B. & S. Glass Co."; the word Sandwich is embossed on the bottom. Because it is the only known pressed Sandwich item marked with the company's name, it may have been an advertising gimmick. *Lafayet* is all that would fit on the allotted space; thus the awkward abbreviation of the ship's name. This blue, opalescent salt container sold for a few cents in 1830; now it might cost as much as **$365**. *From the collection of the Sandwich Glass Museum, Sandwich, Massachusetts.*

Oil Lamp and Spill

This canary-colored, pressed-glass oil lamp is in Sandwich's Star and Punty pattern. A matching spill, for holding the twisted paper tapers used to light the oil, is shown at right. The lamp and spill were made circa 1850. In canary, the spill is a **$200** item today: the lamp goes for twice as much. *From the collection of the Sandwich Glass Museum, Sandwich, Massachusetts.*

Carnival Glass

Carnival Glass collectors have found only one opalescent, aqua-colored punch bowl in this "Peacock at the Fountain" pattern. In June, 1976, it sold at auction for **$9,000**. The pattern was manufactured by the Northwood Glass Company between 1910 and 1920. Punch sets in this pattern in other colors are more common and less expensive. *Photos this page courtesy of Jack and Mary Adams, International Carnival Glass Association.*

People's Vase

The Millersburg Glass Company, which operated a glass factory in an Amish area in Ohio, from 1909 to 1912, produced this piece of Carnival Glass. Known as the People's Vase, it depicts dancers in Amish dress. The vase is 12 inches high and weighs nearly 5 pounds. The People's Vase is legendary among Carnival Glass collectors because only five samples in four different colors are known to exist. All of them have sold at auction in the last four years for prices well over **$4,000**.

Frolicking Bears Pitcher

The crazy energy of the Frolicking Bears pattern is not what inspired someone to pay **$6,000** for this pitcher at an auction in February, 1976. It is rarity that makes it valuable: only three such pitchers have been found to date. One was discovered at a basement sale in Kansas City for **$10**; collectors of Carnival Glass all hope for the same sort of luck.

Lamp Base

The Aladdin Company created an Art Deco oddity when they designed this 14-inch Depression Glass lamp base. Collectors love its strange pinkish glow and, when they can find one, might pay as much as **$500**. *All glass pages 48 and 49 courtesy of As Time Goes By, New York City, unless otherwise indicated.*

Royal Lace Butter Dish

When people began to perceive Depression Glass objects as collectibles rather than junkware, the Royal Lace pattern was the thing that caught their fancy. When Depression Glass collecting took off, many other patterns surpassed Royal Lace in desirability and value. Pictured here, however, is an example of a green Royal Lace butter dish that survived the competition, sporting a **$200** price tag.

Cherry Blossom Depression Glass

A 14-piece child's tea set in the cherry blossom pattern might run **$150**. But take a close look at this pattern, for if you find pink salt and pepper shakers to match it, you've got a 4-figure Depression Glass collectible on your hands.

Manhattan Glass

Pressed "Manhattan" glass-ware was once five-and-dime deco; now it is being snapped up at **$8-$10** per plate–more for the larger pieces–and gaining fast on the more traditional Depression patterns shown on these pages. *Courtesy of Galleria, New York City*.

American Sweetheart Pattern

If you think that sugar bowl lids are expendable, think again. The rare lid pictured here is worth **$150**, while the bowl it covers is a **$5** trifle. This opalescent glass tableware, in the American Sweetheart pattern, is a favorite among collectors of Depression Glass. Sweetheart salt and pepper shakers are also very scarce, so **$150** price tags on the few which are known to exist wouldn't surprise the knowledgeable.

Akro Agate Tea Set

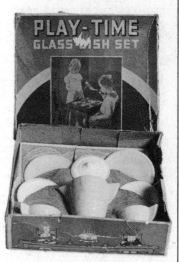

Though a child may hostess a number of teas, she rarely maintains her service as she should. Remarkably, this Akro Agate tea set from the 1930s is still intact in its original box, and collectors are willing to invest **$50** in this plaything.

Useful Tools and Devices

The pursuit of food, clothing and shelter has been keeping people busy for centuries. The tools and utensils which have enabled man to cook, spin thread and build houses are far from frivolous, but people have always managed to color even life's difficult tasks with fun and imagination. Evidence of such spirit is revealed in the brilliant design and detail of the practical paraphernalia of the past. These nitty-gritty wonders appeal as collectibles to the person who appreciates the value of a better mousetrap. Old trade catalogs, many of which are being reprinted, as well as inventories and conversations with older people, are all valuable sources for documenting a tool collection. Many old tools are available for under $10; but those of fine materials like wrought iron, brass and rosewood are priced much higher. But no tool is getting easier to find. For every one discovered, there are many more thrown out by an ill-advised consumer who opts for a new appliance.

Kitchen Utensils: Those for whom the kitchen is the most comfortable room in the house have no difficulty viewing cooking utensils as toys or art objects. The old-fashioned connoisseur of fresh, hot coffee and warm, just-browned apple pie gives due respect to the coffee roaster (p. 54) and the apple slicer (p. 55) responsible for such pleasures. These utensils are not commonly used today and are desirable collector's items. Old egg beaters (p. 53) and nutmeg graters (p. 54) might have accompanied your grandmother's recipe for eggnog pie. You should have saved both, for among collectors, the Edgar Nutmeg Grater is now famous for its scarcity. If you're superstitious, you may believe that bread will rise properly only in a basket inherited from your mother (p. 56). Your irrational thinking is a boon when it's the price of your basket that's rising so nicely.

Sewing Tools: Sewing, like cooking, is viewed as an art by its advocates, and the craft has been the inspiration for a variety of neat gadgets. Sewing birds (p. 57), valued for their forgotten functionalism and graceful lines, have gone up in price to $175. A needle dispenser, encased in a wooden mushroom, is as lovely as it is useful (p. 57). The sewing box, which holds many of these collectible tools, can be a valuable accessory in itself, if handsomely structured with little luxuries (p. 59). Of course, all of these sewing tools are still usable today. More remote are the various contraptions for spinning thread and yarn and for winding them into skeins (p. 60), a skill rarely practiced in the age of manufacturing.

Hand Tools: Old hand tools are usually a bargain, often better designed, heavier, and less costly than new ones. Many tool collectors are enthusiastic craftspeople who find working with old tools more satisfactory. Other collectors are interested in preserving the methods of using a variety of interesting tools that are no longer made today. Tools were brought from England to America on board the Mayflower, and the westward flow has never ceased. In rural areas, where the imported tools were not readily available, most craftsmen had the ability to create a tool for every need. Often these tools exhibit wonderfully decorative touches, which distinguish them from the standard factory-made tools—a caliper with high-heeled boots (p. 62), a plane with a mouse-shaped handle (p. 64), an ivory-barreled bow drill (p. 64). Even barbed wire is collected for its more than 700 designs, and some of the awesome barbs manage to look pretty (p. 65).

Suggested Reading

Andere, Mary. *Old Needlework Boxes and Tools,* Drake, 1971.

Bealer, Alex. *The Tools that Built America.* Potter, 1976.

Franklin, Linda Campbell. *From Hearth to Cookstove 1700-1930.* House of Collectibles, 1976.

Glover, Jack. *The Bobbed Wire Bible #4.* Sunset Trading Post, Sunset, Texas, 1976.

Ketchum, William C. *American Basketry and Woodenware: A Collector's Guide.* Macmillan, 1974.

Salaman, Raphael. *Dictionary of Tools Used in the Woodworking and Allied Trades.* Allen and Unwin, 1975.

Whiting, Gertrude. *Old-Time Tools and Toys of Needlework.* Dover, 1971.

Kitchen Utensils

Egg Holders or Stands

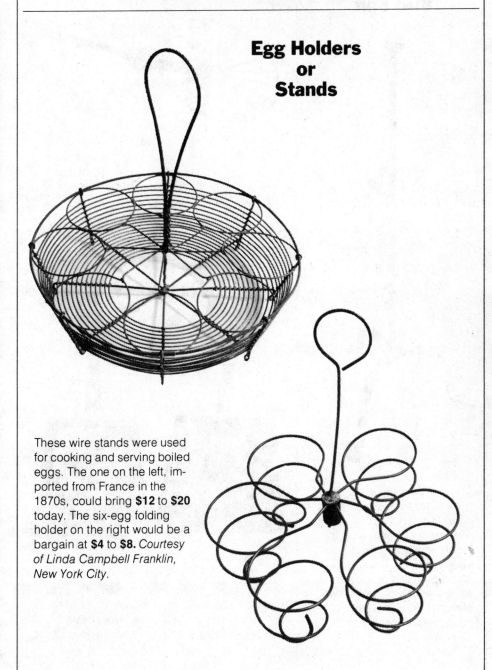

These wire stands were used for cooking and serving boiled eggs. The one on the left, imported from France in the 1870s, could bring **$12** to **$20** today. The six-egg folding holder on the right would be a bargain at **$4** to **$8.** *Courtesy of Linda Campbell Franklin, New York City.*

Adjustable Bird Spit

Rotary Grill

This 18th-century revolving meat broiler, probably American, was set right in front of the hearth, with a pan beneath it to catch the drippings. A lubricating grease cup, located under the pivot, kept the 13½-inch grill spinning smoothly. Today, such an implement would probably sell for **$125-150**. *Photo courtesy of Paul Persoff, New York City.*

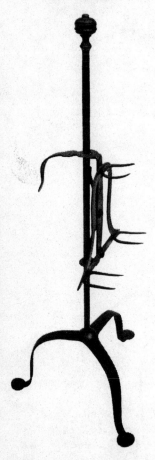

Dust Pans

Three birds or small game animals could be spitted at the same time on this wrought-iron 18th-century stand. After the height was adjusted, the device was placed before the fire. It was sold at auction for more than **$125.** *Photo courtesy of O. Rundle Gilbert, Garrison-on-Hudson, N.Y.*

These wooden-handled dustpans were made by Shakers. Their spare simplicity shows the same understanding of form which is evident in all products of Shaker industry in the late 19th and early 20th centuries. The one on the left was sold at auction for **$75**; the one on the right brought **$110**.

Turbine Churn

This 1870 pine churn made lots of butter. Farm women used large churns like this one; house-wives used smaller, tabletop ones. You can make your own butter for **$65** to **$90** in such a churn. *Courtesy of Farmrest Antiques, Goulds-boro, Maine.*

Meat Chopper or Hasher

Mincemeat pies, hash, and sausage were all made in a cast- and sheet-iron machine like this one, patented in 1865 by LeRoy Starret, in Athol, Massachusetts. Meat was placed in the revolving drum, and the cutting blade rose and fell as fast as the crank turned. This tool sells for **$65** to **$120.** *Photograph courtesy Paul Persoff, New York City.*

Butter and Egg Beaters

With cast-iron gears, tin lids, and glass jars, these utensils beat eggs (top) and churned butter (bottom). Both sold for about $1.75 seventy years ago; today they would cost between **$15** and **$20** each. *Courtesy Linda Campbell Franklin, New York City.*

Coffee Roaster

Around 1880, a coffee roaster like this could have been found over a hole in the top of many kitchen ranges. Made by Griswold Mfg. Co., which manufactured many cast-iron utensils, this roaster would cost from **$25** to **$40** today. *Photo courtesy of Paul Persoff, New York City.*

Coffee Mill

Before the turn of the century, cast-iron coffee mills, often painted red, were found on every country store counter and in almost every kitchen. Today this mill would cost about **$200**. *Courtesy of Fran Faulkner, New Kingston, New York.*

Coffee Percolator

This Art Deco coffee percolator of chrome and plastic, made and signed by Chase, pays service to an era that delighted in sleek, futuristic designs. The **$150** it costs today might buy a ticket to the moon a hundred years from now. *Courtesy of Galleria, New York City.*

Nutmeg Grater

The famous Edgar Nutmeg Grater stores the nutmeg and protects the fingers from the rough grater. The spring holds the nutmeg against the grater while it is rubbed back and forth. Its ingenuity, attractiveness, and relative rarity make this 1891 Edgar worth between **$10** and **$15**. *Courtesy Linda Campbell Franklin, New York City.*

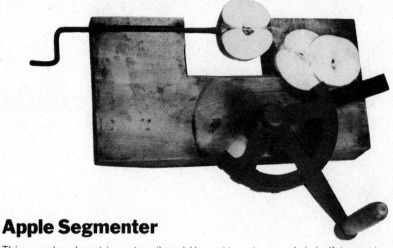

Apple Segmenter

This wood and cast-iron utensil could be set to cut an apple in half, in quarters, or in thin sections for apple pie. Since the apple (stored or made into pies) was a favorite in 19th-century America, it's no wonder this now curious utensil was once a commonplace. Its curiosity value is reflected by its price. This simple device would probably sell for at least **$35-$40** today. *Photo courtesy of O. Rundle Gilbert, Garrison-on-Hudson, New York.*

Can Opener

When this 1889 cast-iron can opener was patented, about 50 million one-pound cans of food a year were being processed in Baltimore, a canning center. This tool cut a hole 2½ inches in diameter in the top of a can. It is worth about **$8** to **$10.** *Courtesy Linda Campbell Franklin, New York City.*

Apple Parer

This apple parer provided sitting space at the end opposite the crank. The cook could slip an apple on one prong and peel it with a twist of the handle. Hundreds of homemade wooden parers, with iron or wood gears, were in use from 1840 to 1900. People even took them to paring bees. The painted design on the one shown here looks Pennsylvania Dutch. Dating from the 1870s, it recently brought **$65** at auction. *Courtesy Linda Campbell Franklin, New York City.*

Fruit-Drying Baskets

These flat splint baskets served as trays for drying fruit, which was an important part of the farm family's diet in the 19th century. Now the trays cost **$25** for the smaller one and an additional **$20** for the larger one.

Shaker Basket

The 19th-century Shaker community in Hancock, Massachusetts, designed this 10-inch-wide splint basket for collecting the morning's fresh eggs. The finely carved handle adds elegance to the already fine craftsmanship apparent in all Shaker items. Shaker designs are sought after today, and baskets are among the most desirable. This one goes for **$125**.

Rye Straw Basket

Palatine German settlers in the New Jersey-Pennsylvania area used rye straw to make baskets like this one. The rye was twisted and coiled into basket shapes and held together with strips of heavy cord or hickory bark. This shallow basket held rising bread dough. Since rye straw baskets are unusual, they're valued at **$35**. *Courtesy of Stone House Antiques, Lexington, New York.*

Sewing Tools

Sewing Bird

Sewing clamps were used in the first half of the 19th century to hold one end of a piece of material to the table, so that the fabric could be pulled taut for stitching. The most ingenious of all sewing clamps was the sewing bird, which held material tightly in its beak. To move the material, the operator depressed the bird's tail and the beak would open; the clamp itself never had to be unscrewed from the table's edge, as it did in the more common clamp forms. This cast-iron clamp is valued at **$175.** *Courtesy of Stonehouse Antiques, Lexington, New York.*

The Practical Stocking Darner and Needle Case

The Practical Stocking Darner and Needle Case was more than practical, it was a sewing wonder. Socks could be darned over the rounded wooden mushroom cap. When the top was removed, one had only to dial the size number of the desired needle and the small hole on top would release that needle from the storage stem. These services are dear today; this sewing tool goes quickly for **$60**. *Courtesy of Tender Buttons, New York City.*

Stocking Darner

Stocking darners are traditionally humble tools, but not this one. Dating from 1890, this beautiful souvenir from Luzerne is elegantly constructed of inlaid woods and has the appearance of a tightly constructed wooden puzzle. Such crafts- manship in a simple tool brings **$40** today. *Courtesy of Tender Buttons, New York City.*

Thimble and Thread Holder

This 4-inch souvenir of Mount Washington, New Hampshire, was probably purchased for Grandmother for a few cents in 1890. Such kind thoughts re- quire a more serious commit- ment now — **$35.** *Courtesy of Tender Buttons, New York City.*

Pin Cushion

This beaded, strawberry-shaped pin cushion, filled with rosin and topped with velvet, is a **$60** sewing artifact. Two inches high, this pin cushion dates from the 1870s. Pin cushions are a popular collectible, and strawberries a specially favored shape. *Courtesy of Tender Buttons, New York City.*

Pin Cushion and Spool Holder

A Shaker craftsperson made this wooden pin cushion and spool holder. Wire dowels, which have been removed, held spools on the two lower levels. Like all Shaker work, this sewing accessory is well constructed; it sells for **$150**. *Courtesy of Stonehouse An- tiques, Lexington, New York.*

Amish Sewing Box

A characteristic feature of Amish settlers in Pennsylvania is their special clothing, all homemade, plain, and without buttons. It is not surprising that their sewing equipment has always been well constructed and highly functional. This painted, 13-inch sewing box provides easy access to a variety of spools and has storage space for tools and threads. It is quite rare and valued at **$225.** *Courtesy of Stonehouse Antiques, Lexington, New York.*

Niddy-Noddy

"Niddy-noddy, niddy-noddy, two heads; one body" chanted a 19th-century spinner as she held this tool in the middle and wound wool from end to end. The chant helped her keep up an efficient winding speed. Niddy-noddys are not rare, but this one, with its turned spindle and hand carving, was unusual enough to bring **$40** at auction.

Sweet Grass and Willow Sewing Basket

The Penobscot Indians of Maine began, in the 19th century, to use a marsh grass called sweet grass for making baskets, which they still sell to tourists. Here, sweet grass is woven with willow to give the basket strength and rigidity. Today, collectors will buy it for **$20.** *Courtesy of Confetti Iman, Cherryfield, Maine.*

Swift

This unusual wooden swift was used for winding thread or yarn in 19th-century households. The latticework expands and contracts so that the circumference of the skein can be controlled. When fully expanded, the device measures about 2 feet wide. It is valued at **$100.**

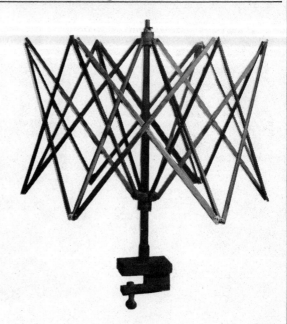

Clock Reel

After thread or yarn was spun from fiber, it was measured and wound into skeins on this clock reel. From the top of the wheel to the floor, this implement measures 48 inches. It was common in 19th-century households and is valued now at **$50.** *Courtesy of Burnham Tavern, Machias, Maine.*

Spinning Wheel

This flax wheel from Indiana was commonly used in the 19th century for spinning linen thread from which clothing was woven. The 36-inch-high wheel is now valued at **$125.** *Courtesy of Old Salt House Antiques, West Gouldsboro, Maine.*

Hand Tools

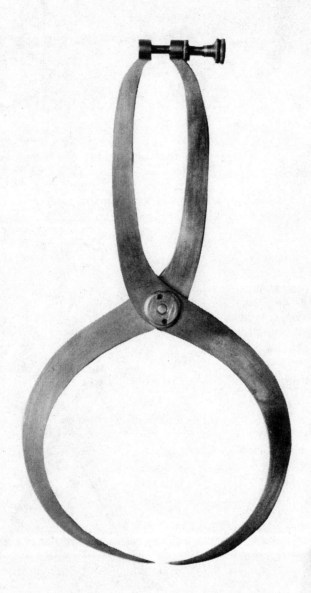

Stove Maker's Calipers

Handmade brass calipers were used to insure uniform thickness of the wood master pattern for the cast-iron walls of ornate Victorian woodburning stoves. These rather large late-19th- or early-20th-century, fine quality calipers cost from **$75** to **$100**. *All photos pages 61-64, unless otherwise indicated, from the collection of Daniel Semel.*

Bit Brace

This late-18th-century bit brace has a clothespin bit pad so that different size bits can be inserted in it. The decorative scalloping and chip carving suggest Scandinavian origin, although it may have been made in Vermont or New Hampshire. Because it is very old and in fine condition, it is worth between **$175** and **$225**.

Traveler

This early-19th-century tool was used by wagon or coach makers to measure the circumference of a wheel. Because it was cast, not forged, and has an unusual design, with a liberty-capped handle, this tool might bring close to **$125**.

Calipers

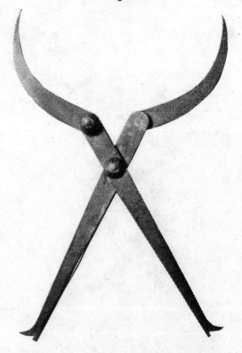

This 20th-century tool measured inside and outside dimensions of cylindrical or round objects. Called "dancing master" calipers in England, this one-of-a-kind "Esquire"-legged tool is valued at **$20.**

Hay Knife

This forged iron, 19th-century hay knife, which resembles a saw, was used to cut slices of hay out of a mow for cattle feed. It cost 62¢ in 1895 and about **$35** now. *Courtesy of Jonesport Wood Company, Jonesport, Maine.*

Snow Hammer

This hand-forged iron hammer was used as a pick for removing snow and rocks from horses' hooves. It hung by its clip from the sleigh, so that it was ready when needed. It is a late-19th-century tool valued between **$25** and **$50**.

Cabinetmaker's Scraper

This tiger maple scraper was drawn or pushed across a piece of cabinetwork, and a thin shaving of the surface was removed. The brass-wear plates assured a flat surface. The scraping blade could be sharpened over and over. The depth of the shaving was determined by how much blade was pushed through the slot. Dating from the second half of the 19th century, it is valued between **$50** and **$75**.

Clockmaker's Hacksaw

The tightness of this tool's 3½-inch blade is adjusted by a tension nut. This well-made tool conforms to the Lancastershire pattern and was designed in England in the late 18th or early 19th century. In good condition it is worth about **$25**.

Sheet-Metal Dial Gauge

Before the introduction of micrometers, dial gauges like this one were used to measure the thickness of thin sheets of precious metals like silver and gold. A millimeter's difference from the measurement claimed might have meant a lot of money. This brass gauge from the second half of the 19th century is worth about **$50**.

Bow Drills

Fine bow drills of ivory, ebony, rosewood, steel, and brass have a history dating back to 8000 B.C. These two (dated about 1870-1890) have come a long way from the first adapted bow-and-arrow drill. Both handles, the ivory (left) and the rosewood (right), are removable for adjusting tension and thereby regulating speed. The rosewood-handled drill, with an ivory barrel, was made by Napoleon Erlandsen, a New York City machinist. Each drill is worth approximately **$200**; a bow costs **$100**.

Miter Shooting Plane

This unusual birch plane, with original wedge and "Mickey Mouse" handle, is typical of 18th-century New England design. The maker's mark is J. Fisher. The gouge marks on the side, the 22-inch length, and its fine condition make it worth between **$100** and **$150**.

Round Molding Plane

Caesar E. Chelor, who died in 1784, was the first black planemaker. He was the slave of the first documented American planemaker, Dean Francis Nicholson (1683-1753), who freed Chelor in his will. Chelor closely followed Nicholson's designs and made cabinet- and woodworkers' planes like this molding plane. A uniquely American plane of birch and hand-forged iron, this historically significant tool is worth from **$100** to **$150**.

Barbed Wire

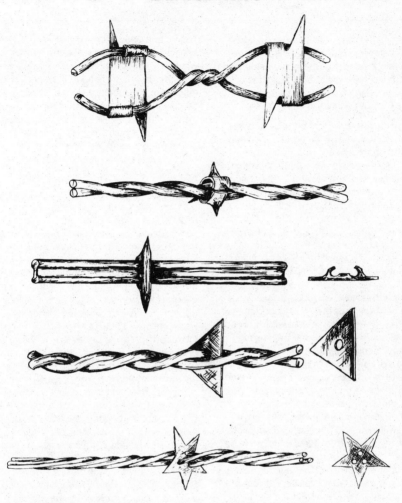

During the last ten years, many serious collectors of barbed or "bobbed" wire have been searching for unknown types of wire that are still wrapped around fence posts. Eighteen-inch lengths called "sticks" sell from 25¢ to over $300 apiece. The types of wire vary from twists to two-wire strands, with a simple barb every seven or nine inches, to complicated "obvious" designs, which made the barbs easily visible and therefore less dangerous to livestock. Some barbs are intricate, thorny knots; others are sheet-metal clip-ons. Many sticks are available to the collector for under **$10,** but the prizes of any collection are the rarities. From top to bottom: Elsey Plate, patented July 18, 1882, **$100**; E.S. Wheeler Spike Collar of June 30, 1885, **$90**; Scutt's Webbed Ribbon, October 23, 1883, **$30**; Pond's Triangle from January 2, 1883, **$120**; and the Hart-McGlin Star patented September 12, 1876, **$300**. *Illustrations courtesy of C.W. "Smokey" Doyle, Texas Barbed Wire Collectors Association, Fort Worth, Texas.*

Packaging and Politics

Packaging, be it an idea, a product, or a politician, is something uniquely American. We practically invented modern advertising, and perhaps modern politics as well. Antiques associated with these activities are now choice items among collectors.

Advertising Art: At the turn of the century, the country store was a mythical place – a neighborhood hub where anyone could stop by to pick up some gossip with a pound of coffee. Patrons gazed at shelves lined with brightly colored tin canisters containing everything from tobacco to flour. Often, the tins bore no labels; a familiar shape or motif identified the contents clearly enough, and recycling was encouraged. A series of "Roly Poly" tins, for example (p. 67), which held Mayo's tobacco, were meant for re-use as brownie tins. Undoubtedly, the appealing series was collected then as well as now. But today, a collector might pay hundreds of dollars for one empty Roly Poly. Country stores were kept supplied with advertising gimmicks, all bearing the generous donor's name. A handy string dispenser (p. 70), for example, kept customers aware of the ubiquitous Heinz pickle. A stack of manufacturers' catalogs, displayed on the countertop, were there to thumb through, too. Sometimes called "wish books," illustrated with pictures, prices and descriptions, they listed hundreds of items which could be ordered: handtrucks, roses, stoves, tractors, artificial limbs, boxes, clocks and pens, to name only a few. Now, even the catalogs are collected (pp. 72-73). Attractive advertising posters were tacked to every available surface depicting folk heroes, like Buffalo Bill (p. 71), enjoying American-made goods with a satisfied air. Often these posters were made to last of lithographed tin, much to the joy of contemporary collectors who will pay hundreds of dollars for unusual examples in good condition (p. 70). Today, one pays dearly for what was once given away. For example, trade cards, which were distributed freely on the streets to bombard the public with an advertiser's message, sell today for 50¢ to $5 (p. 71). And outside the store, all along Main Street, trade signs beckoned. Many are now considered folk art (p. 10). In many American towns the local soda fountain was illuminated by stained-glass Coca-Cola chandeliers.

Today, authentic ones are among the highest-priced advertising collectibles to be found – if you can find them (p. 69). But not every advertising rarity is an antique. There is a commonplace commodity which is collected seriously and even traded at conventions. It's the lowly beer can. Not any old beer can, of course. But if you have chug-a-lugged a can of Playmate Beer (p. 68) and thrown the can by the wayside, then you have cause to regret your littering.

Politics: Packaging and promoting a candidate for political office has become a continuously refined American art since the 1860s. One of the first political buttons of the pin-back variety was made for Abraham Lincoln's campaign and bore his photograph (p. 74). Today it commands the respectable price of $150. One might assume that such antiques are the most valuable, but buttons dating from the campaigns of Theodore Roosevelt (p. 74) and FDR (p. 74) are bringing the record-breaking prices today. The value of a political item is based on a candidate's popularity. Of course, scarcity and demand are the overriding factors that cause prices for campaign memorabilia to soar. Locally produced buttons and delegate buttons often become scarce because fewer are produced than those distributed by national campaign headquarters. Scarcity also results when the supply of a relatively common button is mysteriously depleted, as with the McCarthy TV Screen (p. 76), perhaps through the efforts of zealous campaign clean-up committees. Political items are sold and traded regularly at conventions and through mail-order auction catalogs. Collectors' clubs like the Association for the Preservation of Political Americana (p. 190), are dedicated to preserving and researching authentic items, and weeding out counterfeits, called *brummagems*.

Suggested Reading:

Clark, Hyla M. *The Tin Can Book*, New American Library, 1977.

Grossholz, Roselyn. *Country Store Collectibles Price Guide*, Wallace-Homestead, 1972.

Hake, Ted. *Encyclopedia of Political Buttons, 1896-1972*, Dafran House, 1974.

Klug, Roy. *Antique Advertising*, 3 volumes. L-W Promotions, 1972.

Advertising Art

Roly Poly Inspector

The Inspector, or Man from Scotland Yard, is the rarest of the six Roly Poly tobacco tins made by Tindeco in the early 20th century. Inspectors in mint condition like this one have sold for as much as **$500**. The five other tins of the series, in descending order of rarity, are: Satisfied Customer, Dutchman, Singing Waiter, Storekeeper, and Mammy. All were made to contain Mayo and Dixie Queen tobacco. *From the collection of Lester Barnett, San Francisco, California.*

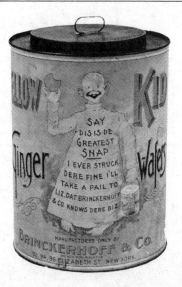

Yellow Kid Tin

The Yellow Kid was created by New York cartoonist Richard Outcault in 1894. The Kid's reactions to his situation were always written on his yellow gown. It was the first comic strip printed in color and eventually made Outcault famous. The container stands over 18 inches high and is the only known Yellow Kid tin of its kind. The label is paper, and the price? "I wouldn't trade it for three Cadillacs," says its owner. *From a private collection.*

Friends Tobacco Tin

When Dad finished the tobacco in this reusable tin, the youngsters carried it to school as a lunch pail. Dating from the early 20th century, this Friends tin is increasingly more difficult to find. Consequently, prices have soared. Examples in good condition now sell for as much as **$250**. *From the collection of Lester Barnett.*

Playmate Beer Cans

The Sunshine Brewing Company of Reading, Pennsylvania, manufactured Playmate beer and malt liquor for a brief period in 1966. Legend has it that the brewery was sued by *Playboy* Magazine, who claimed *Playmate* as their own trademark. A collector interested in this rare can might be willing to pay as much as **$100** for it. *From the collection of John Ahrens.*

Tin Moxie-Mobile

Moxie, you may recall, was a soft drink popular in America in the 1920s. It guaranteed energy and power. The phrase, "He's got a lot of moxie," was a compliment back then, and the gentleman in the one-horsepower vehicle was intended to convey the message. This advertising toy's curiosity value brought **$240** at auction.

Pawnbroker's Sign

This New York City pawnbroker's sign of the 19th century is a fine example of advertising art. Three golden balls are the traditional symbol of a pawnbroker's shop, and these retain much of their original gilt. The overall dimensions of this piece are 36 inches by 45 inches. It is valued at over **$800**. *Ed Weissman, Antiquarian, Portsmouth, N.H.*

Coke Change Receiver

At the turn of the century, almost every soda fountain had a change receiver located near the cash register. Because they were made of glass, relatively few of these items have survived. As a result, they are prime collectibles. The one shown at left is considered the most valuable of them all. Measuring 8¼ inches in diameter and depicting the famous actress Hilda Clark, the glass tray dates from 1901. It is valued at over **$1,000** today. *Photo at left, and below, left, courtesy of the Coca-Cola Company.*

Tiffany-Type Coca-Cola Chandelier

The Coca-Cola Co. issued this 15¼-by-12½-inch chandelier between 1905 and 1920. The dome panels and the trademark are white opaque glass; the trademark panel is ruby red stained glass. The ornate metal band near the top reads "Property of the Coca-Cola Co. To be returned on demand." The likelihood of anyone returning one today is slight; such pieces have sold for more than **$2,500**.

Trade Cards

The different poses of these cherubs induced many people to collect the whole delightful set of five in the 1880s. Stock trade cards like these were sold to a variety of merchants, who printed their own names and addresses on them. Thus, all five of these die-cut fans advertise Frank B. Clark's stationery store, but the same fans may be found spreading a different organization's fame. In the last few years, the cards have risen remarkably in price to nearly **$5** each. *From the collection of Lester Barnett.*

Vienna Art Plate

A museum portrait? Hardly. This framed, lithographed tin plate was an advertising giveaway at the St. Louis Exposition of 1904. Imitating fine Viennese china on the front, it spread Anheuser-Busch's message on the back (detail at right). In mint condition and framed, it could bring **$70** at flea markets these days. *From the collection of Judy Hazelcorn.*

Butcher's Sign

This 19th-century, well-wrought pig is indeed superior among trade signs. The phrase "Pork Butcher" indicates the British origin of this carved wooden piece, while the **$750** auction price reflects an appreciative American market.

Heinz Pickle Sign

Country store proprietors hung this clever Heinz string dispenser in a prominent spot, usually near the pickle barrel. An excellent example of tin advertising memorabilia, the dispenser reminded all customers of Heinz. The plate above bears the famous "57 Varieties" slogan. Dispensers of all kinds are valuable collectibles. This one, complete with original string, is a lucky find for less than **$600**.

Sapolin Enamel Sign

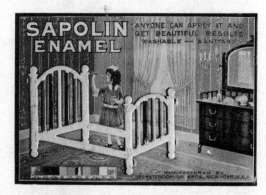

This embossed tin sign is no more than 7 inches by 10 inches, yet **$250** would be a modest appraisal of its value to collectors. The bed's three-dimensional effect, the rainbow of brilliant colors being painted on it, and the overall excellence of the sign's condition contribute to its desirability as an example of advertising memorabilia.

Cigarette Poster

In the 19th century, Old Judge Cigarettes used contemporary celebrities to draw attention to their product. They reasoned that if Buffalo Bill liked their cigarettes, then everybody would. Prince Albert and the prize fighter, John L. Sullivan, are also part of this circle of smokers, all of whom learned the habit from the Indian seated on the right. This 20-by-12-inch advertising poster would sell for at least **$85**. *Courtesy of Old Museum Village, Smith's Cove, Monroe, New York.*

Lord and Taylor Business Card

Is Baby Frog showing sheer delight or fear of the unknown because of new stockings from Lord & Taylor? No matter for Mama Frog looks wise. She knows good merchandise. This 3-by-5-inch advertising card was given away by the famous New York store in the 1880s. Today, collectors pay **$5** for it. *Courtesy of Brandon Memorabilia, N.Y.C.*

Tobacco Advertising

When this 19th-century transformation card is folded shut, it reveals an ugly old woman with a sour expression. When the card is opened, the lady becomes the picture of beauty and contentment. In the accompanying verse, the makers of mild-smelling Virgin Leaf implied that women prefer sweet-smelling kisses to foul tobacco breath. Today, the card is worth **$5-$8**. *Courtesy of Brandon Memorabilia, New York City.*

Trade Catalogs

Slack's "Everything for Amusements" Catalog

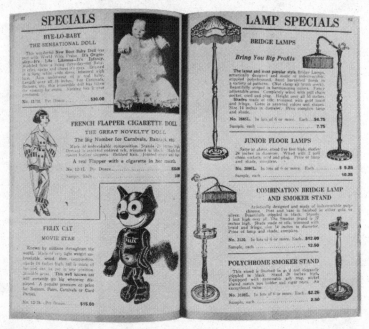

Many small, amusing and easily-destroyed novelties which bring high prices now are pictured in this flimsy 1920s catalog. Made for carnivals or parties, items like squawker balloons or celluloid dolls once sold for pennies. Today the catalog alone sells for **$5-$10**. *All catalogs pages 72 and 73 from the collection of Linda Campbell Franklin, New York City.*

Bradley's Kindergarten Material & School Aids Catalog

"A trained kindergartner will not be satisfied with inferior material," announced this 1904 catalog of learning "gifts." Perforated sewing cards, colored-paper parquetry, toy knitters, and a handsome cabinet of weights and measures were aids for teachers. This sparsely illustrated catalog costs between **$5** and **$10**.

L. Reusche & Co. Catalog

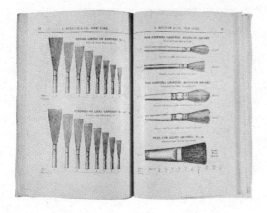

This artists' supply catalog advertises air brushes, printing presses, and china painters' supplies. Pictured inside are some brushes, dusters, blenders, stipplers, shaders, and tracers sold around 1920. Like many catalogs, this one includes a list of useful books printed at the back. This catalog sells for **$6**, but its value keeps increasing.

The National Flag Company

The 45-star American flags featured inside this catalog date it between 1896 and 1907. The catalog advertises bunting, flag holders, and novelties like parade ammunition canes (which were protected from spontaneous combustion). The patriotic subject and the four-color printing make this catalog worth between **$10** and **$15**.

E.T. Barnum Iron & Wire Works Catalog

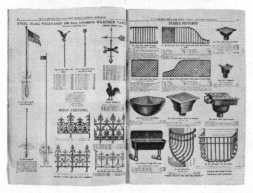

At the turn of the century, architects selected grilles, sturdy partitions, or roof crests in the form of royal crowns as decorations for stores, banks, offices, barns, and cemeteries. This 1923 catalog even offers steel lockup cells. Other pages feature canopies, porticoes, and fire escapes. Dealers specializing in catalogs sell these architectural catalogs for between **$7** and **$18**.

Political Buttons

Bull Moose Pin

A jugate is a pin that pictures the presidential and vice-presidential candidates. This one of Theodore Roosevelt and Hiram Johnson is suspended from a gold delegate pin by a red, white, and blue ribbon. The pin recalls President Roosevelt's unsuccessful 1912 presidential campaign on the Bull Moose Party ticket and sold for **$3,165** at auction. *From the mail auctions of George H. LaBarre Galleries, Hudson, N.H.*

Rare Cox-Roosevelt Button

This rare jugate is a memento of the only election Franklin D. Roosevelt ever lost. In 1920, Governor James Cox of Ohio ran for president and FDR, Assistant Secretary of the Navy, ran for vice-president against Warren G. Harding. They lost by a landslide. Very few of these buttons were issued in the low-cost campaign following World War I. Because so few are available, they are valued between **$2,000** and **$4,000**. *Photo courtesy of Ben Corning, Framingham, Mass.*

Devil Doll

Press on the foot of this Grover Cleveland, nickel-plated watch fob, and the hand in his pocket moves up to thumb his nose while a devilish tail pops out from behind. The 1⅝-inch fob, called a devil doll, was made for the Blaine-Cleveland campaign of 1884. It sold at auction for **$375**. *Courtesy of George Rinsland, Allentown, Pa.*

Lincoln Ferrotype

This Abraham Lincoln ferrotype—a photograph printed on a thin iron plate—was made in 1864. The photograph is mounted on a pin back, which is standard for modern-day political buttons but rare for such an old button. This pin is valued at **$150**. *Photo courtesy of Foster B. Pollack, New York City.*

Military Insignia

No one knows exactly how this badge, picturing Ulysses S. Grant, was originally used. Perhaps it was a campaign badge during Grant's run for the Presidency; perhaps a veteran of the Civil War wore it as a patriotic gesture. It is made of silvered brass and measures 1¼ inches by 3½ inches. The large pin consists of an eagle, an anchor on a blue ribbon, a shield bearing the brass-framed ferrotype of Grant, and a Boys-in-Blue banner. The pin sold at auction for **$612**. *From the mail auctions of George H. LaBarre Galleries, Hudson, N.H.*

Rare Lincoln Silk Ribbon

A large bust of Abraham Lincoln is printed in black ink on this silvery-blue silk ribbon. The 2⅜-by-7¾-inch ribbon is in mint condition, and commemorates the 1860 Lincoln-Hamlin campaign. The ribbon sold at auction for **$415**. *Photo courtesy of George Rinsland, Allentown, Pa.*

Mechanical Goldbug

Push the tail of this mechanical goldbug and the wings, with pictures of William McKinley on the left and Garret Hobart on the right, pop out. The goldbug symbolized McKinley's 1896 support of the gold standard. Today, the pin is estimated at **$125**. *Courtesy of Foster B. Pollack, N.Y.C.*

FDR Delegate Button

FDR delegates wore this 1¾-inch button in 1932. The button is surrounded by a satin rosette with red, white, and blue ribbon streamers suspended from it. Finery like this does not go unrewarded. The button is currently worth between **$300** and **$500**. *Courtesy of Foster B. Pollack, New York City.*

Greeley Head Fan

This fan, depicting Horace Greeley, was created by his opponents in the presidential campaign of 1872. A number of anti-Greeley cartoons decorate the back. It sold at auction for **$61**. *From the mail auctions of George H. LaBarre Galleries, Hudson, N.H.*

TV-Screen Button

This 1½-inch button bearing a TV-screen image of Eugene McCarthy is a recent but rare political button. Not many of these buttons were manufactured in 1968, and very few are in existence today. The gray and blue button could command **$75-$100** from collectors. *Courtesy of Foster B. Pollack, New York City.*

Taft-Sherman Jugate

This 1¼-inch jugate supported Taft and Sherman in the 1908 election. The button, a rarity because it was issued only in Bloomington, Illinois, sold at auction for **$550**. *Photo courtesy of George Rinsland, Allentown, Pa.*

Getting Around

Collectors are making the concept of planned obsolescence obsolete. Bicycles and automobiles, easily abandoned for newer models, are being retrieved, rebuilt and pampered by those who see them as valuables, not junk. Individuals can hardly collect trains and steamships, but passengers and operators have salvaged hardware and souvenirs from the stately old lines. By replacing the seat on an old bicycle (p. 79), by "appropriating" dining-car china (p. 84), by bidding at auctions sponsored by bankrupt rail or steamship lines, collectors are recycling the transportation industry — to great personal advantage.

Bicycles: Bicycles, the people-powered vehicles, have been a useful and popular conveyance since the 19th century, when even eminent Victorians mounted highwheelers. Today, in good condition, they are selling for $500 and up. The safety bike (p. 79), which followed the highwheeler, was more rideable and less expensive; it began the first populist bicycle craze in the 1890s, a boom unequaled until the 1960s, when riders became enchanted with the 10-speed bike. But even a fine, modern European bicycle may be less costly than the restored version of that old, safety bike your great-grandfather left in the shed.

Automobiles: More seductive than any ride on a bicycle-built-for-two were those spins through town in the family's new Chrysler 300A (p. 82). If you still have that huge, chromed cradle of your youth, you're in luck. Cars produced after World War II are fast becoming collectors' treasures; some sell for more than the original sticker price. Whereas classicists worship awe-inspiring radiators and elegant coachwork, the new breed of car collector seeks sportscars — like the 1963 Chevrolet Corvette (p. 82), and the 1955 Ford Thunderbird (p. 81) — which reflect that period's emphasis on speed and styling.

Railroads: Railroad employees have had the best opportunity to collect most of that industry's souvenirs. A conductor who may have inadvertently left a badge (p. 84) or a set of keys (p. 83) in his bureau drawer, always found a spare the following day. A switch lock (p. 83) or lantern (p. 84) may have been taken as a self-awarded retirement gift by the person who had access to the storeroom. However it happened, much official railroad hardware now rests in the hands of collectors, who seem driven to acquire items from each of the numerous national and local lines. Short-lived lines and the numerous, local shortline companies provide the rarest collectibles.

Steamships: In the years after World War I, a first-class ticket for a transatlantic ride on a luxury liner was indeed a luxury. But once aboard, there were inexpensive souvenirs aplenty — razors (p. 86), spoons (p. 86), notebooks (p. 87), even flower vases (p. 86). These items were meant to be saved for sentimental rather than economic reasons, but if you weren't a packrat then, it's your financial misfortune now. Today, a paper menu from the "Normandie" commands $15 as a reminder of by-gone luxury (p. 87). The persistent search for steamship memorabilia will keep a collector's enthusiasm afloat long after his favorite ship has been retired.

Suggested Reading

Automobile Quarterly, 245 West Main Street, Kertztown, Pennsylvania 19530.

Car Classics Magazine, P.O. Box 547, Chatsworth, Georgia 91311.

Klamkin, Charles. *Railroadiana,* Funk and Wagnalls, 1976.

Palmer, Arthur Judson. *Riding High, The Story of the Bicycle,* E.P. Dutton, 1956.

Smith, Robert A. *A Social History of the Bicycle,* American Heritage Press, 1972.

Wagenvoord, James. *Bikes and Riders,* Van Nostrand Reinhold Co., 1972.

Bicycles

Tandem Quadricycle

This Coventry Club Tandem, made in England in
1886, is the ultimate vehicle for elegant country
cruising. The metal frame and hard rubber tires
are propelled by the two large wheels. The quad-
ricycle can be steered and braked from either
front or rear, so the riders have every option for
division of labor and seating arrangement. The
small back wheel is attached to the body by a
movable joint and goes from side to side as well
as up and down when scaling bumps in the road.
This was an expensive bicycle when it was
made, but today, at **$6,500**, it costs more than
some automobiles.

The Sociable Bike

The unique design of this "sociable" tandem places the riders side by side, with room between for an umbrella or a baby's seat. Both riders pedal and steer. Made by the Punnett Cycle Company in the 1890s, this variation of the bicycle-built-for-two was never very popular and was soon discontinued, making this a very rare collector's bicycle. Today it costs **$1,500**.

The First Safety Bike

In the 1890s, bicycle manufacturers developed the chain and gear drive so that large-circumference wheels were no longer necessary. Immediately, the size of the wheel shrank, and the new bike was marketed as a safety bike, because the rider sat low between two wheels rather than riding precariously over the front axle. The safety bike started history's first big bicycle craze in the 1890s. This first safety bike, with hard rubber tires, is worth **$750**.

Boneshaker

This early bike, with iron tires on wooden wheels, was nicknamed the "boneshaker" because of the bumpiness of the ride. These bicycles appeared in the 1860s, predating the discovery of the comfort of rubber tires. A hand brake, attached to a very thin cable, is operated on the handle grip. Before this bicycle was restored with paint and a leather seat, it cost **$400**. In its present condition, it is worth much more.

The Eagle

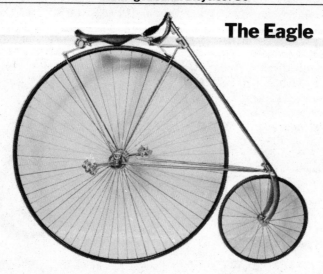

The Eagle Manufacturing Company made this high-wheeler unusual by putting the large wheel in back. The rider must start the bike rolling and then mount the rotating pedal, which carries him up to the seat atop the back wheel. This makes the bicycle difficult to learn to ride. Built in the 1880s, the great period of the highwheeler, the bicycle was customized with a nickelled frame, enamelled wheels and spokes, and a leather seat. Prices vary greatly for highwheelers, but this one, in restored condition, costs **$3,000**.

Columbia Tricycle

This two-track Columbia tricycle was made in 1885 by the Pope Manufacturing Company, a large manufacturer of American bicycles still in business today. Tricycles were used for business as well as pleasure by doctors and mail carriers of the period. This one was designed for a woman — there is no bar to clear before sitting, and the mesh covering protected skirts from the chain. This tricycle is valued at **$4,500**.

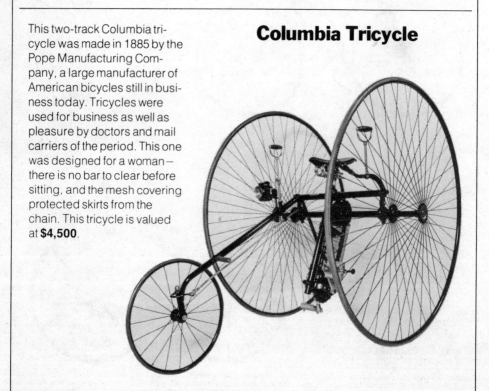

Automobiles

1951 Nash Healey

It is unlikely that an owner of this Anglo-American car would be unaware of its rarity. The English chaise was designed by Donald Healey, who also lent his name to the Austin Healey. Models have sold for as much as **$10,000**. *Photos pages 81 and 82 courtesy of the Long Island Automotive Museum, Glen Cove, New York.*

1955 Ford Thunderbird

The 2-passenger Ford Thunderbird was the first personal car designed in America in many years. Made only from 1955 to 1957, the 2-seater model has remained a super-star and constantly surpasses its original $2,500 sticker price. In 1975, models sold at auction for **$6,000-$7,000**.

The 1955 Chrysler 300A

The Chrysler 300 series was the first postwar production-line car with over 300 horsepower. It featured a large Chrysler engine, hemispherical combustion chambers and an Imperial grill. The series began in 1955 with a limited edition which broke all the stock car records. Subsequent models were identified by a letter. The series ran from the 1955 300A through the 1961 300G. All letter cars are valuable, but the A model is the most valuable because of scarcity. Models have sold for as much as **$7,000**, depending on their condition.

1963 Studebaker Avanti

The car collectors' claim that nothing worth collecting has been produced since 1960 is refuted by the 1963 Studebaker Avanti. The Raymond Loewy Studios put a fiberglass coupe around a modified Lark engine to make this fast-moving and exciting design. The Studebaker Corporation collapsed shortly afterwards, but other companies continued to manufacture these cars calling them simply "Avanti." Although subsequent models look like the original, the Studebaker remains the one most sought after, selling for **$4,000-$6,000** today.

1963 Corvette Stingray

A split rear window dates a Corvette Stingray as the vintage 1963 model. Noted for its speed and performance, the Stingray appreciated in value from its original $4,000 sticker price. An unrestored (original paint) 1963 model sold recently at auction for **$6,800**, placing this car in the **$5,000-$7,000** range today.

Railroadiana

Switch Locks

Used to lock up switches along the right-of-way, these brass padlocks were opened by specially-issued keys. The heart shape and embossed, rather than incised, RR markings, as well as the good condition, make these locks worth **$15-$20**. Keys, showing wear but if "nicely used," bring **$4-$20** depending on rarity. *Photos pages 83 and 84 (except bottom right, page 84) courtesy of Scott Arden's Railroadiana Shop, Noti, Oregon.*

Badges

Until badges and uniforms were introduced, RR employees were indistinguishable from passengers. Cap and breast badges, usually of brass and nickel plate or colorful enamel, and buttons identified conductors, watchmen, brakemen, ticket collectors, station agents and other workers. Badges showing occupation and RR name sell for **$15** and up. Uncommon job titles or lines add value.

Dining Car China

Railroad dining car china and silver-plated flatware, usually marked with the line's name, are highly prized. This 2¾-inch-high, heavy china creamer is scarce because it is marked "Pullman." It might sell now for **$7-$15**; a dinner plate of this pattern could cost **$60** in mint condition.

Dietz Railroad Lantern

Conductors gave the go-ahead with this early-20th-century Dietz kerosene lantern by snapping the green lens into position. The shield in front of the lantern made for a clearer signal by allowing the lantern's glow to pass only through the interchangeable lenses. The price tag on this lantern might be **$100**. *Courtesy of Old Museum Village, Smith's Cove, Monroe, New York.*

Steamship Memorabilia

Transportation Poster

At the port of Le Havre, the arriving train deposits passengers at the boarding ramp of the steamship which will carry them to New York. The Compagnie Générale Transatlantique, France's prestigious steamship line, asked the noted marine painter, Albert Sebille, to design this approximately 2⅓-foot by 4-foot poster around the turn of the century. Brightly colored in red, white, and blue, his design captures the excitement of an impending departure. Depending on condition, this poster could be worth as much as **$150**. *All items, pages 85-88, courtesy of Carl House.*

Souvenir Medals

Medals like these were often given to favored passengers as souvenirs. The medal on the right, from the Hamburg-America's *Amerika*, is valued at **$60**. The medal on the left, from the *Normandie*, is stamped 1933 and signed by Jean Vernon, who designed many decorative medals of this type. This one is valued at **$125**.

Chrome Vase

This elegant vase from the *Normandie* is valuable as a piece of steamship memorabilia and as a fine example of Art Deco. Made of chrome on brass, it was designed by Edgar Brandt, an important Art Deco artist noted for his work in wrought iron and bronze. A collector could easily expect to pay **$400** for one of these 14-inch beauties.

Souvenir Razor

Shaving on board ship can be hazardous if the seas are choppy. If you have a steady hand, you might like to try this souvenir razor from the turn of the century. It is inscribed from the American Line with an etching of the *St. Louis* on the blade. Today, this razor could cost up to **$20**.

Souvenir Spoon

Souvenirs from luxury liners took many forms; some were practical and some simply decorative. This spoon is from the Hamburg-American Line's *Deutschland*, launched at the turn of the century. Made of enamel and gold plate, this spoon is valued at **$15-$20**.

Ile de France Brochure

Any devotée of Art Deco will be enchanted with this brochure describing the *Ile de France*. Blue and silver tones provide a festive cover for this booklet, which contains color plates of the interior of the ship. It is valued at **$40**.

Menu from the Normandie

The term "luxury liner" was certainly appropriate as can be seen in this photograph of the *Normandie*'s dining room. The elegance of the environment was equaled only by the cuisine. This menu is valued at **$15**.

Silver Notebook

If you would like to take notes of your sea cruise, this silver notebook might come in handy. The Hamburg-American Line made this souvenir for its ship the *Amerika*. Originally sold for $3.50, this notebook costs up to **$50** now.

Queen Elizabeth Launch Brochure

On Sept. 27, 1938, the famous *Queen Elizabeth* was launched, and this elegant brochure was issued in celebration of the occasion. The naming ceremony was performed by the Queen Mother. King George VI was unable to attend, so a letter of apology was included in the brochure. This brochure, containing photos of celebrities attending the ceremony and shots of the construction process, is worth over **$100**.

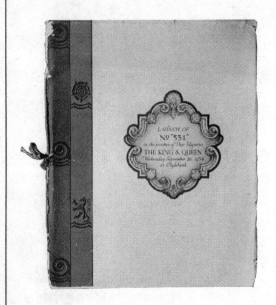

Queen Mary Launch Brochure

"A Masterpiece in the Making" is the title of the text of the launch brochure of the *Queen Mary*, and indeed she was a masterpiece of construction. The first British ship to exceed 1,000 feet, the *Queen Mary* also captured the Blue Ribband as the fastest ship to cross the Atlantic. Her mean speed was 31.7 knots; the previous record of 31.2 knots was held by the *Normandie*. The brochure contains signed, fold-out lithographs of the shipbuilding in process, shown below. The project was titled No. 534, as the name of the ship was kept secret until the launching. Today the brochure is valued at **$100-$150**.

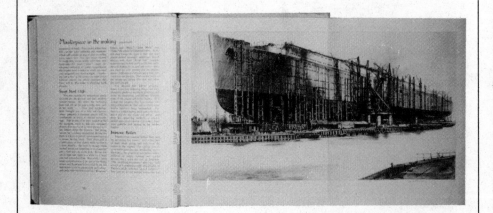

Posting a Message

A good letter deserves re-reading – that's the motivation for stuffing a year's worth or more of letters and postcards into a shoebox. But one rarely pulls them out again, and the shoebox eventually gets shoved to the back of the attic. One hardly anticipates that a stranger may not only read his personal mail someday, but sell pieces of it for large sums of money. Everyone knows that stamps are collected avidly. What everyone doesn't know is that old letters, postcards, and especially old envelopes can be quite valuable as well.

Stamps and Covers: When mails were carried by stagecoach, steamship, and railroad, people waited weeks to hear from relatives who had left to settle new territory; months before word arrived from missionaries en route to China. Because American immigrants had personal ties to the Old World, letters flowed freely between the continents. Letters from the major European capitals were very common, but one written from an unusual location is quite valuable today (p. 91). In those early days, letters were simply folded and posted – no stamp or envelope was necessary. The U.S. Government first issued postage stamps in 1847; since then, stamps have commemorated every variety of person, place and event. Removing a stamp from its "cover," as postmarked envelopes with attached stamps are called, can decrease its value by 95%. For it is not only the stamp, but the postmark (p. 91), the place of origin, the addressee, or a forwarding signature (p. 90), which can contribute to a cover's worth. In the 1930s, collectors attached Graf Zeppelin stamps to self-addressed envelopes and postcards to gather the postmarks which the dirigible's mail cargo received at each port-of-call. Today, a Graf Zeppelin cover is worth $400 to the person who bothered to send it to himself.

Postcards: The Government postal card, first issued in 1873, allowed brief open messages to travel for 1¢, a rate lower than that of letters. The idea caught on and postcards were sent by the millions. Picture postcards, which appeared in 1893, were published by commercial printers. Cards printed prior to 1907 are distinguished by the absence of a divider line on back. Only the address could be written on the blank back. Messages had to be squeezed on the front. Postcard designs encompassed a broad scope. Almost every small town had postcards printed showing its train depot or a prominent building. Now, the more obscure the town, the more a collector will pay for its old postcards. Postcards honoring early airplanes (p. 95), election results (p. 94), and world's fairs (p. 94) were collected to be enjoyed as a parlor entertainment. The collecting craze died with World War I, only to be recently revived. Cards that sold for a dime five years ago are now bringing $5 and up.

Greeting Cards: Greeting cards have experienced the same phenomenal appreciation, and the prices being paid have nothing to do with extravagant holiday spirit. A Christmas card designed by Kate Greenaway, England's famous 19th-century commercial artist, is priced at $20 or more these days. A valentine collector will buy a handmade lacy card from the 1860s any day of the year, and you can be sure he won't send it off to his sweetheart. In America, several prominent figures mark the beginning of commercially-made greeting cards. The German immigrant Louis Prang, known as the father of the American Christmas card, perfected a chromolithographic (color) printing process, which gave his studio's cards the popular and artistic edge in the 1870-80s (p. 99). Esther Howland, an American woman, hired a bevy of workers to assemble delicate bits of ribbon, lacy papers, and colored pictures into the first commercial valentines (p. 97). The surviving work of these early greeting card producers is a paper nest egg for those who had the foresight to collect them just a few years ago.

Suggested Reading:

Buday, George. *The History of Christmas Cards*. Printed in England by Richard Clay. Chaucer Press, 1965.

Lee, Ruth Webb. *A History of Valentines*. Lee Publications, 1962.

Miller, George and Dorothy. *Picture Postcards in the United States 1893-1918*. Crown, 1975.

The Scott Monthly Journal. Scott Publishing Co., 530 Fifth Avenue, New York, New York 10036.

Stamps and Covers

Graf Zeppelin Stamps

On April 19, 1930, the U.S. government issued three denominations of stamps celebrating the flight of the Graf Zeppelin from Germany to the United States. An envelope's round trip from New York to Germany via boat, and then from Germany to New York on board the Zeppelin, cost $2.60. This cover, as stamped envelopes are called, was autographed by passengers and crew members of the Zeppelin, which adds to its value. In the midst of the Great Depression, it was decided that these stamps were too expensive. They were withdrawn on June 30, 1930, and unsold quantities were destroyed, making these short-lived stamps very rare. This interesting cover sold at auction for **$375** in 1976. *All photos pages 90-92 courtesy of Kover King, Inc., N.Y.C.*

Folded Letter

The sender of this 1766 letter had no idea that it would become a valuable collector's item when he gave it to a friend to carry by hand from Jamaica to New York. In New York, Mr. Phil Livingston picked up the letter and forwarded it through the mails to the addressee, by marking the back of the folded letter, which went without envelope in those times. Later, Philip Livingston signed the Declaration of Independence, and this autographed evidence of his role as the middleman makes the letter a **$400** collector's item.

Missionary Letter

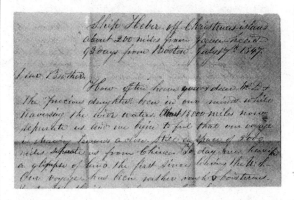

Letters from exotic places are quite valuable. If a letter has a postmark or heading that shows it was written in a place where few literate people lived, it is obviously a rarity. This letter, sent from the Indian Ocean by Bostonian missionaries on their way to China in 1847, is a collector's item with a **$500** price tag.

Chicago Shield Postmark

In the late 19th century, every local postmaster was free to design his own canceling device; the fancy blue Chicago shield makes this postcard worth about **$50.** Before canceling became uniform, thousands of postmarks were created, and they have cash value today. Without the postmark, this card would be worth a dime, even though it is from the first edition of the government-issued postcards.

Romagna Stamps

The stamps on this envelope are from the state of Romagna, which had a short existence before the unification of Italy. Because it was quickly incorporated into Italy, Romagna produced its own stamps for only a brief period, and the stamps are extremely rare. The fact that they are still attached to the original envelope contributes to their **$3,000** value.

Decorated Stationery

The first page of this stationery tells the story of the California Indians to the receiver of this letter. Inside, there is space to fill with more personal news. In the 19th century, the Indians were a subject of great national interest. Collectors still consider anything concerning the Indians a very desirable item; thus, the **$375** value of this sheet of paper.

Charles Magnus Lettersheet

During the Civil War, people liked to embellish their letters with patriotic songs of support for the army. Charles Magnus, a very famous publisher of the era, offered 10 illustrated songs on 5-by-7-inch note paper for 50¢. Now this single sheet, depicting a Civil War battle scene and ballad, might sell for **$20**.

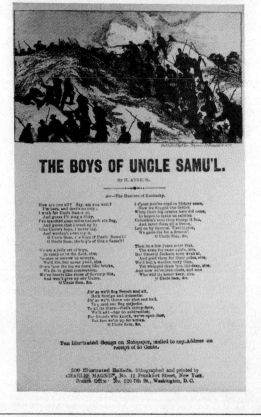

Postcards

Novelty Postcard
This delightful novelty post-card, made in 1910, is a hand-tinted photograph. The lady's coiffure is made of real human hair pasted onto the card. The card is valued at **$10.** *All post-cards pages 93-96 from the collection of Mary L. Martin, Glen Burnie, Md.*

University Girls
This smiling coed is from a series of six postcards titled *University Girls.* It was made in 1907 by the English firm Raphael Tuck and Sons and is valued at **$8.**

Coin Card

This postcard from Mexico shows different coins from that country. It was made in 1905, is embossed, and is valued at **$15.**

"Hold-to-Light" Card

This souvenir of the 1904 St. Louis World's Fair is a hold-to-light card. It has translucent spaces, which make the windows of the building seem to light up when the card is held up to a light. It is valued at **$25.**

Political Postcard

Many collectors specialize in one topic, such as politics or presidents. This 1908 postcard of William H. Taft is a **$20** rarity.

Fire Engine Postcard

Disasters were often pictured on postcards. This card from 1905, titled *Going to the Fire,* shows a steam-operated fire engine. It is valued at **$5.**

Early Dirigible

Postcards were printed to celebrate special events, heroes, and inventions. Pictured here is Roy Knabenshur's air-ship, which he attempted to fly in 1905. The card costs **$15.**

Early Train

In the early part of the century, almost every city or town, no matter how small, had postcards made of local historical events and points of interest. This postcard from Central City, Colorado is valued at **$6.**

Early Aviation

This postcard shows the *Spad*, a famous type of French World War I fighter plane. Made in 1910, this card is valued at **$20.**

Early Western

Collectible as a postcard and a photograph, this 1911 card, *The Chiefs at the Roundup,* has No. 82 in the lower left-hand corner, indicating it was one of a series. Sets of postcards were common in the early 1900s, but they were not always numbered, so there is no sure way of knowing how many cards were in a series. This card is worth **$10.**

Fourth of July Card

In the years preceding World War I, patriotic spirit was high, and America's birthday was adequate inspiration to greet friends and family with a special postcard. This brightly colored, embossed card is one of a set of six Fourth of July cards and might cost **$10** today.

Christmas Card

The Santa Claus shown here is wearing a red satin appliquéd suit. In 1910, it cost only a penny to have this Santa bring his Christmas greetings; today you could spend as much as **$30** to send him through the mails.

Greeting Cards

Esther Howland Valentine

Esther Howland launched her valentine business in 1847, the year she graduated from Mount Holyoke College. Her cards, in the style of English hand-decorated valentines, were produced with the help of an assembly line of female workers. This inset picture with a lace border is typical of her work. Embossed with the initials of Howland's New England Valentine Co., the card is valued today at **$15** and up. *All cards pages 97-99 courtesy of Brandon Memorabilia, New York City.*

Valentine

Though its origin is not known, this valentine from the 1850s resembles the lithographed bird designs of Dobbs, Kidd, & Company, a London stationer, bookseller, and publisher. The embossed and perforated lacy border, surrounding a decorative center medallion, was very popular in England between 1840 and 1860. This example is worth **$20-35**.

Sachet Valentine

Victorians loved sachet valentines. Perfumed cotton was sewn into a small satin pillow, which was then wrapped in embossed lacy paper and decorated with colorful pictures. Shown at left is a triptych sachet. The card today is valued at **$15-20**.

Kate Greenaway Card

Kate Greenaway is one of the most famous 19th-century commercial artists, and her beautifully drawn children are instantly recognizable. This Christmas card is one of her early works, done for Goodall of London before she began her long association with Marcus Ward and Company of London. The signed card is colored in pale blues, greens, and grays. Kate Greenaway's cards are now selling for **$25** and up.

The Children and the Flowers

This four-part Christmas card, called *The Children and the Flowers*, from Marcus Ward and Company of London, displays more of Greenaway's designs. The card's four panels are colored with pictures of the four seasons; on the back of each, there is a relevant verse. Ms. Greenaway's characteristically beautiful children endear this card to collectors, who will pay **$20-25** for it.

Prang Christmas Card

Louis Prang's interest in the Christmas card was focused on pictorial design and lettering. Acceding to popular Victorian taste, he made his larger cards available with or without silk-fringed borders. As with all of Prang's best work, today it is impossible to attach a single value to this 1880s card. Prang cards range from less than **$1**, in the hands of the uninformed, to over **$100** in the appreciative hands of knowledgeable collectors. No doubt they will continue to increase in value as Prang's fame grows.

1st Prize Prang Card

Louis Prang attracted the country's most talented artists to his enterprise by sponsoring open competitions for Christmas card designs and offering huge cash prizes to the winners. Pictured above is the 6¾-by-8¾-inch card which won first prize in both the popular appeal and artistic excellence categories in 1881. The artist, Dora Wheeler, won $2,000 for her design. The card was a big seller then; a collector's item now.

The Boston Card

L. B. Humphrey, the designer of the Boston Card for Louis Prang, was one of the first female book illustrators in the United States. On the front of the card, a colorful lithograph portrays a Christmas scene; the back, printed in monochrome, provides the message and a view of Boston, thus giving the card its name. Prang's early cards were blank on the back, but from 1880 on, monochrome decorations filled the reverse side.

Words and Images

Books: A family's bookshelves, stocked by generations of readers, can sometimes be fertile hunting grounds for valuable books — from desirable first editions by modern authors to 19th-century illustrated narratives about the Far West and the Civil War. Quite possibly, Faulkner's *Mosquitoes* (p. 104) has been resting quietly on your shelf against *The Marvellous Country* (p. 103) for years without arousing your suspicion. A book can be valuable for many reasons: most often, because of an author's popularity; for its subject matter; or because of its illustrative material. As ideas, authors and artists go in and out of vogue, values fluctuate. One can keep abreast of current trends and prices by periodically reviewing *American Book Prices Current* (listed below), attending auctions and reading bookdealer's catalogs. In the case of modern authors, only the first printing of a first edition usually has value. In addition, assuming the book is in demand and copies are scarce, the valuable copy should have its original dust jacket in good condition. Without it, the book is worth decidedly less, even if the author is as popular as Hemingway (p. 103). Since first editions are not always marked "first edition," it is sometimes necessary to determine a book's publication date through the publisher, rare book dealers, or the card catalog of the public library. This date should agree with the date on the title or copyright page. Two dates usually indicate a second edition or second printing. If your book is indeed a first edition, consider its condition next. Every tear, tatter or scribble detracts from value. Of course, a famous author's inscription, valuable in itself, can sometimes compensate for other damages. Good condition is especially unusual in children's books, so a pristine copy of *The Knave of Hearts* (p. 102) would be a true find. Books concerning the settling and development of the West are generally designated as "Western Americana," a subject of great contemporary interest to book collectors. Condition always remains a consideration in determining value, but historical content and illustrations are also of prime importance. Hand-colored engravings are particularly desirable. Books containing actual photographs were sometimes produced in limited editions in the 19th century, before printing methods allowed text and illustrations to be printed together. Individual plates from such a book, *Photographic Views of Sherman's Campaign* (p. 116), for example, are very valuable both historically and artistically. Even books and journals containing photogravure prints (mechanically printed photographs) by famous photographers like Edward S. Curtis (p. 115) are treasured by both collectors of books and photographica. The prices cited for the books on the following pages are either auction or retail. Generally, a bookdealer will pay from 35% to 40% of the retail price for a book. This is called the A.B.P. (average buying price). This and other abbreviations used in bookseller catalogs are defined in *The ABC of Book Collecting*, listed below.

Images: Because unique works of art, such as paintings, are usually so costly, most people choose to buy the more affordable graphic arts, also known as prints. These can include posters, original prints (as described below), and even antique maps. A distinction is made between a print and a reproduction: a mechanically printed and relatively worthless copy of an existing work of art. As with books, prints are valued either by way of the artist's reputation, or because of the desirability of a particular genre, landscapes, or still lifes, for example.

Posters: The art of the poster blossomed in France in the 1880s and '90s when Jules Cheret and the painter Toulouse Lautrec began designing advertisements for theaters and cabarets. The medium appealed to many artists whose posters are now in museum collections. Printed by lithography, this "art of the streets" has always been collected avidly. Today, those in the Art Nouveau and Art Deco styles are especially sought after. The chances of finding the classic Vienna Secession poster, shown on page 105, are slim; but if you were in Paris in the 20s, you might have purchased one for very little. It has become valuable as examples have become scarce. Posters by known artists will always be the most highly regarded, but even anonymous works that advertise things as commonplace as cigarettes (p. 71) are valued either for what they promote, or the graphic treatment of the subject matter.

Original Prints: Since posters, however beautiful, are always created for advertising purposes, they are considered commercial art and quite distinct from original prints, regarded as fine art produced with a purely esthetic intent. Today, the term "original print" is used to describe a work of art, designed and executed by the artist, using any one of many printmaking techniques by which an impression is made on a flat surface (usually paper) from a fixed plate. Engraving, lithography, and woodcut are some of the traditional printmaking methods. The total number of impressions taken from a single plate is called the edition. In modern prints, of the type shown on pages 108 and 109, editions are deliberately limited and numbered. The artist's signature, in pencil or ink, on each impression usually connotes his personal approval of the work. Prints were not numbered until the late 19th century, so it is impossible to determine the edition for prints made earlier. But in some cases, Currier & Ives' hand-colored lithographs (p. 111), for example, it is known that the editions were large. While such prints sold originally for a few dollars at most, today some are worth hundreds, even thousands of dollars. They are valued as examples of Americana and because particularly desirable prints have become scarce. In assessing the value of any graphic work, be it a poster or original print, condition is of prime importance. Trimmed margins, tears and stains can render a potentially valuable print almost worthless. Also, the quality of different impressions of the same image can vary widely. So an experienced and educated eye — usually that of a museum expert or reliable and established dealer — is the best judge of whether you do, in fact, possess a valuable work of art. When attempting to sell a print to a dealer, expect to receive, at most, ⅓ of the current market value which is set by auction sales.

Photographica: Since its invention in the first half of the 19th century, the photographic image has proliferated in diverse forms. Daguerreotype, ambrotype, calotype and stereoview are just some of the early types of photographic prints. Recognizing these images and the cameras which made them (p. 119) has proved profitable for individuals who have sold their discoveries for impressive, well-publicized sums. For example, a daguerreotype of Edgar Allen Poe was sold in 1976 for $17,000; an anonymous "occupational" (p. 117) brought over $2,000 at auction. The fact that even photographs by unknown photographers are sold for hundreds of dollars at major auction galleries is encouragement enough to become knowledgeable and begin tackling the shoeboxes full of prints that abound in flea markets, where many of these rarities have been found.

Photographica also includes books, journals, and limited-edition portfolios (pp. 115, 116) which sometimes contain valuable prints. Copies of *Camera Work*, Alfred Stieglitz's famous photographic journal (p. 115) are valued for the gravure prints featured in each issue; certain issues could provide a retirement bonus for the foresighted collector who stored them away for a rainy day.

Suggested Reading

American Book Prices Current, 5 year index, 1970-75. American Book Prices.

Carter, John. *ABC for Book Collectors,* rev. ed. Knopf, 1963.

Gernsheim, Helmut and Alison. *The History of Photography*. Thames and Hudson, 1969.

Gilbert, George. *Collecting Photographica*. Hawthorn, 1976.

Hillier, Bevis. *Posters*. Stein and Day, 1969.

Lister, Raymond. *How to Identify Old Maps and Globes, 1500-1850.* Bell, 1965.

Loche, Renee. *Lithography.* Van Nostrand Reinhold, 1971.

Lothrop, Eaton S., Jr. *A Century of Cameras.* Morgan and Morgan, 1973.

Rinhart, Floyd and Marian. *American Daguerrian Art.* Clarkson N. Potter, 1967.

Schmidt, Hermann, Ed. *Paris 1900, Masterworks of French Poster Art.* G.P. Putnam's Sons, 1970.

Stern, Harold P. *Master Prints of Japan.* Harry N. Abrams, Inc., in Association with The UCLA Art Council and Art Galleries, Los Angeles, 1969.

Welling, William. *Collector's Guide to Nineteenth Century Photographs.* Macmillan, 1976.

Zigrosser, Carl. *Prints and their Creators: A World History.* Crown, 1974.

Zigrosser, Carl, and Christa M. Gaehde. *A Guide to the Collecting and Care of Original Prints,* Sponsored by the Print Council of America. Crown, 1965.

Books

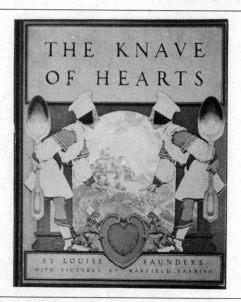

The Knave of Hearts

Glorious illustrations by Maxfield Parrish put this classic oversized children's book on a special shelf. Of interest to children's book collectors and Parrish fans alike, it was written by Louise Saunders and published in 1925. A first edition title page imprint reads: "N.Y. Chas. Scribner's Sons MCMXXV." Anything less than **$200** for this rarity is a steal. *Courtesy of Swann Galleries, Inc., New York City.*

Uncle Remus

Br'er Rabbit, stamped in gold, sits comfortably in his briar patch on the green cloth cover of this first edition. The title page reads: "N.Y. Appleton and Company, 1, 3, and 5 Bond St. 1881. By Joel Chandler Harris with illustrations by Frederick S. Church and James H. Moses." There have been many reprints of this favorite storybook, but it takes a first edition in excellent condition to realize **$125** at auction, as this one did. *Courtesy of Swann Galleries, Inc., New York City.*

A Texas Ranger

Tucked away on many bookshelves at the turn of the century, this 1899 first edition is now a rare book dealer's prize. Valued at **$100-$125**, it features a pictorial, green cloth binding. It is one of the early books published on the American Southwest, an area which is the subject of great interest today. *Courtesy of Argosy Book Shop, N.Y.C.*

American Fairy Tales

L. Frank Baum wrote more than just the Oz books. In one of his lesser-known books, shown here, the title page relates: "Cover, title page, and borders designed by Ralph Fletcher Seymour. Illustrations by Ike Morgan, Harry Kennedy, and N. P. Hall, Chicago, New York. George M. Hill Company, 1901." This first edition sold for as much as **$100** at auction. *Courtesy of Swann Galleries, Inc., New York City.*

The Marvellous Country

Author Samuel Woodworth Cozzens subtitled his handsome book "Three Years in Arizona, and New Mexico, the Apaches' Home." Published in Boston in 1873, it enthralled many an armchair traveler with its 27 illustrative plates and 532 pages of adventurous narrative. This first edition is easily a **$100** book today. *Argosy Book Shop, New York City.*

A Farewell to Arms

All Ernest Hemingway first editions fetch high prices due to the author's enduring popularity. This copy of *A Farewell to Arms,* bearing his autograph on the title page and the original dust jacket in mint condition, is currently estimated at **$500.** A small number of copies of this same first edition carry a note on the fictitiousness of characters, upping its value to **$600.** *House of Books, Ltd., New York City.*

Mosquitoes

A dust jacket can make a $100 difference in the value of first editions. The books shown at right are identical first editions of *Mosquitoes*, a William Faulkner novel published in 1927. The one on the left, in its usual jacket, fetched **$900** at auction; the other, with a less usual jacket that shows a blasé bridge foursome aboard ship, brought **$1,000**. *All items this page courtesy of Swann Galleries, Inc., New York City.*

Jack Kerouac's First Novel

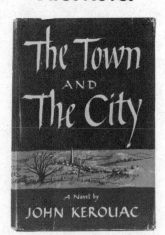

Before Jack Kerouac gained fame as prophet of the beat generation with the novel *On the Road*, he wrote *The Town and The City*. A first edition of his first novel, published by Harcourt Brace & Company in 1950, has brought as much as **$60** at auction when accompanied by its original dust jacket.

The Savoy: an Illustrated Monthly

The Savoy was a fine British periodical, edited by Arthur Symons and published in the late 1890s in London. Contributors included Beerbohm, Dawson, Yeats, Conrad, and many other luminaries. In addition, it was profusely illustrated by Aubrey Beardsley. These six copies, July through December, 1896, brought more than **$150** at auction.

Posters

The Secession

The Vienna Secession was a movement of a group of artists away from the conservatism and provincialism of the Austrian art establishment at the turn of the century. Members worked at a broad range of artistic endeavors, including the applied arts, and looked to artists in other European capitals for inspiration and support. Koloman Moser, a founder of the Secession, designed this poster for the group's fifth exhibit in 1899. The poster's historical importance and beautiful Art Nouveau design make it worth **$4,200**. *All posters pages 105-107 courtesy of Reinhold-Brown Gallery, New York City.*

The Fledermaus Cabaret

Members of the Secession often met for drinks and conversation at the Fledermaus, a cabaret in Vienna. Sometimes they participated in theatrical performances there. Berthold Loeffler, a member of the group, designed this poster for the Fledermaus in 1901. Loeffler's work commands over **$1,000** today.

French Cabaret Poster

Paul Colin did many French cabaret posters. This stunning example of his distinctive Art Deco style was done for a fancy ball in Paris in 1927. The black woman on the poster was inspired by Josephine Baker who, at that time, symbolized all that was elegant and exciting in Paris. It is valued at over **$2,000**.

Life Insurance Poster

Jan Toorop, a Dutch artist of the Art Nouveau period, did this poster for a life insurance company in 1900. Artists rarely ventured into the realm of commercialism, but when they did, the results were usually spectacular. This 37-by-27-inch poster is valued today at over **$1,000**.

Cassandre Poster

The French commercial artist Adolphe-Mouron Cassandre is best known for the posters he designed for the transportation industry. Working in Art Deco style, he transformed railroad tracks and steamships into striking abstract images that are much sought after today. This poster, considered his masterpiece, was done for the French railway line which ran from Paris to Amsterdam, and is valued at **$1,300**.

Costume Ball Poster

The French painter Auguste Herbin designed this poster for a seasonal costume ball, "Dance of Ursa Major," organized by Russian artists living in Paris in 1925. The Big Dipper incorporated in the geometric design symbolizes the name of the dance. Because the poster marked a one-night event, it was probably printed in a small edition, which makes it even rarer today and raises its value to over **$1,800**.

Bordeaux Poster

Jean Dupas, a French Art Deco painter and muralist, designed this 1937 travel poster advertising the seaport, monuments, and wines of the city of Bordeaux. Today, Dupas' alluring poster could sell for **$750**.

Prints

In the depths of the Great Depression in 1934, Associated American Artists, a gallery and publisher of prints, instituted a revolutionary program in an effort to stimulate the market for prints by foremost American artists. Signed original prints, issued in editions of 250, were offered for only $5 each. In some cases, due to lack of interest in a particular work or because something happened to the plate or stone, full editions were never completed. Artists whose works were offered in the original series included, among others, Thomas Hart Benton, John Steuart Curry, Grant Wood, and Ivan Albright. Six works could be purchased for only $25, and, during the height of World War II, a $25 war bond (which cost $18.75) could also be used as payment. As a result, those who took advantage of this program might have purchased all of the prints on this page and opposite for a little more than $3 each. *All photos this page and opposite courtesy of Associated American Artists, New York City.*

Thomas Hart Benton (1889-1975)
Frankie and Johnnie

Published in an edition of 100 in 1936, this lithograph gives a forceful rendering of the climactic scene from the popular blues ballad derived from Missouri folklore. The print, measuring 22⅛ by 16⅜ inches, sold in 1960 for $75; in 1971 for $525; in 1976 for $1,000. It is now valued at **$1,900**.

Grant Wood (1892-1942)
Tree Planting Group

Born in Iowa, Wood painted there all his life and is considered a pioneer in the movement toward regional art. His famous painting *American Gothic* is at Chicago's Art Institute. This, his first lithograph, was published in an edition of 250 in 1937. It measures 8½ by 10¾ inches and sold for **$750** at auction.

John Steuart Curry (1897-1946) Circus Elephants

Like Thomas Hart Benton and Grant Wood, Curry was a leader in the regionalism movement of American art. A Kansan, he painted scenes from local mythology, the circus, landscape, and sports. All his work expresses the tremendous energy of American life. This print, published in an edition of 250 in 1936, measures 9 by 12¾ inches. Its current estimated value is **$750**.

Ivan Albright (1897-)
Self-Portrait— 55 Division Street, 1947

In 1965, the Whitney Museum in New York City mounted a major retrospective show of this Chicago-born artist's paintings, drawings, and lithographs. This lithograph, published in an edition of 250 in 1947, measures 14⅛ by 10 inches and is currently valued at **$1,200**.

George Caleb Bingham Engraving

Large, hand-colored engravings copied from paintings were an important part of American printmaking between 1825 and the Civil War. The paintings of George Caleb Bingham, a principal recorder of American frontier and political life, were a favorite subject of engravers. Because the custom of numbering prints did not begin until the late 19th century, it is not known how many were made. It is known, however, that much of Bingham's work was sold through the American Art Union. But unlike the actual paintings, these engravings were not considered important at the time and many were destroyed. *The County Election,* pictured above, was engraved in 1854 by John Sartain and published by Goupil & Co., New York. It measures 22 by 30 inches and its current estimated value is about **$2,250**. *Courtesy of David Tunick Inc., N.Y.C.*

Winslow Homer Wood Engravings

Winslow Homer (1836-1910) was a foremost American painter of country life and dramatic sea scenes. But he began his career as a freelance magazine illustrator. For over 17 years, his work, in the form of wood engravings, appeared in *Harper's Weekly.* After Homer drew the designs on the wood blocks, they were cut by staff engravers. Bound volumes of *Harper's Weekly* are sometimes found containing full-page Homer engravings, which can range in price from **$50** to **$150.** Seaside scenes, such as *Sea-Side Sketches—A Clam-Bake* from an 1873 issue, shown above, are among his most sought-after designs. *Courtesy of Argosy Book Store, New York City.*

Currier & Ives Lithographs

THE LIFE OF A HUNTER.

Nathaniel Currier and James Merritt Ives formed their partnership as lithographers and "printmakers to the American people" in New York in 1857. Fulfilling their belief that pictures were a necessity of life, they published over 7,000 titles that catered to every taste. Scenes — both sentimental and informative — of American life, winter scenes, views of ships and railroads, western and sporting scenes, and disasters (see page 184) are among their most popular subjects. The prints, designed by artists and hand colored by a dozen or so women in assembly-line fashion, were sold wholesale and retail in three general sizes and ranged in price from 15¢ to $3. Pictures were sold everywhere, through pushcart peddlers on the streets of New York, and country and overseas representatives. The most valuable of all Currier & Ives prints is shown above: *Life of a Hunter–A Tight Fix,* currently valued at **$9,000.** Designed after a painting by A. F. Tait, it was published in 1861 and measures approximately 18 by 27 inches. In general, earlier and dated prints are the most valuable. Prints with margins trimmed to the illustration are worth much less. *Photo courtesy of Kennedy Galleries, Inc., New York City.*

Japanese Wood-Block Prints

In the mid-17th century, a type of wood-block print developed in Japan as the popular art of the emerging middle class. Called *Ukioy-e,* or Images of the Floating World (connoting the Buddhist sense of the transitory nature of human life), they were used as souvenirs, posters, and advertisements; and though much admired and valued today, they were disdained as inferior art by the aristocracy in their time. The most popular subjects for these prints were actors and women, reflecting the popular passion for Kabuki theater and tea houses, where the loveliest courtesans could be found. Landscapes, such as the Hiroshige snow scene at right, became subject matter for prints in the early 18th century. The earliest *Ukioy-e* were printed in black. Red and green were the first colors to be introduced; and in about 1765, polychrome printing appeared. Hundreds of thousands of wood-block prints were produced from 1658 to 1858. It is estimated that in the early 1800s, one would have cost about 25¢. In the late 19th century, they became popular with the French Impressionists and exerted a strong influence on their painting. As late as 1922, a good print could be purchased for $5. In 1948, prints by some of the greatest masters were selling for $500; in 1972, a Hiroshige triptych brought **$14,000** at auction. *Photos this page courtesy of the Ronin Gallery, New York City.*

Hiroshige (1797-1858)
Snow Viewing at Uekiya Mokuboji

The great landscape artists of the wood-block print were Hokusai and Hiroshige. While many of Hiroshige's prints were limited to editions of 200, many were printed in editions of thousands, and it is thought that he designed perhaps 10,000 prints during his life. He did many series of travel illustrations of famous bridges and places in Edo. This print, from the series *Celebrated Edo Restaurants,* was produced between 1835 and 1839. Twenty years ago, it might have sold for $100. In 1975, it was sold for **$600.**

Goyo (1880-1921)
The Model Tomi

The classic period of *Ukiyo-e* ends with the death of Hiroshige in 1858, but Goyo is among the few later artists who embody the classic style. He fully completed only 14 prints during his life and limited editions to 80. This typical courtesan print, in which the woman is completely at ease and unaware of the artist, was produced in 1920. It might have been purchased before World War II for under $100. In 1975, it sold at auction in London for approximately **$2,500**.

Maps

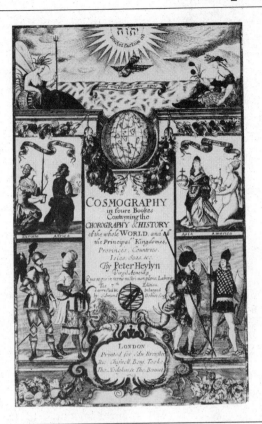

Cosmograph of Peter Heylyn

This title page from Peter Heylyn's *Cosmography* is typical of attempts by early map publishers to make their maps more appealing and saleable by adding decorations to the title page. These decorations often had little to do with the subject matter of the map. Frontispieces and title pages are collected as a specialty because they are usually finely engraved. Made in London in 1703, this title page is valued at **$100**. *All maps from the collection of Paul Roberts Stoney, Lancaster, Virginia.*

Portolano of the Black Sea

Portolanos were sailors' charts, drawn originally by seamen for their own use when they were at sea. This map of the Black Sea, made by Nicolaes Witsen in 1696 in Amsterdam, has one distinguishing characteristic — exaggerated detail of the shore line and the lack of inland detail. Good portolanos are scarce, since they were usually destroyed through constant use. This map is valued at **$350.**

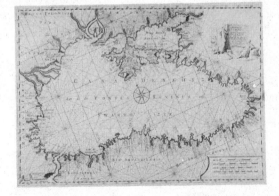

The World

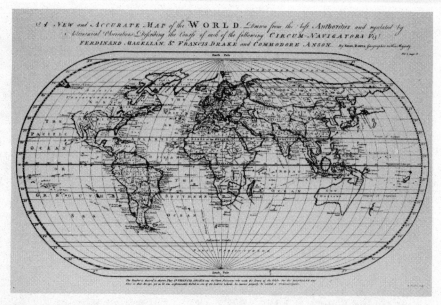

World maps rank first in international popularity. This one was made by Emanuel Bowen in London in 1744. Many early world maps were designed for a specific purpose or event. This map was designed to commemorate the accomplishments of Sir Francis Drake. It is valued at **$250**.

Miniature Atlas

This map of America, made by Hermann Moll in London in 1711, is from a miniature atlas made for the use of travelers. Reducing larger atlases to small pocket size in later editions was a common practice for map publishers in the 17th and 18th centuries. Notice how Moll has followed the popular myth of the time and shown California as an island. Northwest America is simply marked "unknown" and left blank. This map is valued at **$175.**

Photographica

Camera Work

From 1903 to 1917, Alfred Stieglitz edited *Camera Work,* a quarterly photographic journal, shown at left. The work of art photographers of the day was included in each issue in the form of gravure prints. Individual issues are valuable in terms of content. Issue No. 36, which includes 16 photogravure prints by Stieglitz, was sold at auction in 1975 for a record **$5,500.** In the same year, a complete series sold for **$47,000**. *Photos this page courtesy of Robert Schoelkopf Gallery, New York City.*

Edward S. Curtis Gravure Prints

Some of the finest photographs of North American Indians were taken by Edward S. Curtis in the early 1900s. His major work, *The North American Indian*, consists of 20 large portfolios of gravure prints and 20 smaller text volumes, which accompany the portfolios and also contain prints. This Indian portrait from the text volume might sell for **$40-$50.** The large gravure prints sell for **$60** to **$100** each, depending upon subject matter. A record price of **$60,000** was realized in 1975 for a complete set of 20 portfolios and 20 text volumes at the New York auction house of Sotheby Parke Bernet.

The Decisive Moment

The decisive moment
Photographs by Henri Cartier Bresson

In July 1952, Simon and Schuster, in collaboration with Editions Verve of Paris, published this large (approximately 15 inches by 10½ inches) format book of photographs by Henri Cartier Bresson. The cover design is by Henri Matisse. Captions were issued in a separate booklet. Originally a $12.50 book, first editions have sold at auction for as much as **$150**. *Courtesy of Swann Galleries, Inc., N.Y.C.*

Views of Sherman's Campaign

Until a method for printing text and photographs on the same page was perfected at the turn of the century, books were sometimes issued with actual photographs bound into the text. Many of these limited edition volumes, published from 1844 to the 1890s, contain art photographs highly valued by collectors. One of the greatest visual records of the Civil War is contained in such a book: *Photographic Views of Sherman's Campaign,* a folio of 61 10-inch by 14-inch photographs by George N. Barnard, published in New York in 1866. Prints from that book, like the one shown, have sold for as much as **$750**; complete albums cost as much as **$12,000.** *Courtesy of Robert Schoelkopf Gallery, New York City.*

Daguerreotype

A daguerreotype is a photographic image made on a silver-coated copper plate. Because no negative is involved, the image is reversed and unique; one plate makes one daguerreotype and only one. The silvered surface of a daguerreotype reflects light like a mirror, and the image sometimes seems obscured by the glare. Occupational views — portraits of people posing with the tools of their trade — are eagerly sought by collectors. The young man in this 1854 daguerreotype holds a navigational instrument. Such daguerreotypes can range in value from **$150** (for this one) to several thousand dollars (see opposite, above). *Courtesy of Allen and Hilary Weiner, New York City.*

Daguerreotype

This 2½-by-3-inch daguerreotype, called a sixth-plate, was one of the standard sizes made to fit inside cases. Undoubtedly, this is the last word in occupationals: a daguerreotype of an unknown daguerreotypist posing with his camera; his hand is focusing the lens. In 1976, this daguerreotype was sold for **$2,500.** *From the mail-order auctions of George La Barre Galleries, Hudson, New Hampshire.*

Ambrotype

Ambrotypes, like daguerreotypes, are positive and unique images, but they are taken on glass rather than on silvered metal plates. This ambrotype portrait by the famous Civil War photographer Mathew Brady was made in 1857 and is valued at **$100**. Ambrotypes are usually found inside miniature cases; the latch of this case appears at right. *Courtesy of Allen and Hilary Weiner, 392 Central Park West, New York City, dealers in Antique Photography.*

Waterfall

One rarely finds a daguerreotype of an outdoor view. Because such elaborate preparation was necessary to capture a daugerreotype image, most daugerreotypists settled for studio work. This 1854 landscape therefore is valued at **$400**. *Courtesy of Allen and Hilary Weiner, New York City.*

Mascher Stereoscope Daguerreotype

In 1852 John F. Mascher marketed a daguerreotype folding case which could be held like binoculars so that two images could be viewed stereoscopically. This portrait of an unidentified man, made in Philadelphia c. 1853, is framed in such a case marked with Mascher's name. It sold at auction for **$250** in 1976. *Photo courtesy of Martin Gordon, Inc., New York City.*

Railroad Stereoview

Railroads were a 19th-century phenomenon and are still a popular category of stereoview collecting. This fine shot of the Central Pacific Railroad is worth **$15**. *Courtesy of Allen and Hilary Weiner, New York City.*

Civil War Stereoview

In 19th-century America, before newspapers were able to reproduce photographs, stereoviews were education and entertainment. The Civil War was ripe subject matter in 1862, when this stereoview was taken. It depicts Major General Burnside (in the tall hat) and Mathew Brady, the period's most famous photographer (in the porkpie hat). The fact that Brady is pictured increases the value of this stereoview to **$125**. *Courtesy of Allen and Hilary Weiner, New York City.*

Stereoscopic Camera

Stereoviews were photographed with a dual-lensed camera like this one from around 1860. This stereo wet-plate camera is constructed with extendible bellows for focusing. A plate of ground glass covers the back and serves as viewfinder. This camera sells for **$1,200.** *Courtesy of Allen and Hilary Weiner, New York City.*

Stereo Viewer

This French stereo glass-slide viewer revealed 3-dimensional wonders through its eyepieces. By turning the crank at the left, a person could see, in succession, 25 glass slides. Glass stereoviews were more popular in Europe than in America, where photographers began producing large numbers of card stereoviews by 1860. After the stereoview went out of vogue, this machine, which is 20 inches high, was considered junk. Now collectors will pay **$500** to own one. *From the collection of Howard Hazelcorn.*

The Kodak

The Kodak, manufactured in 1888 by the Eastman Dry Plate and Film Co., was the first camera to integrate roll film. The winding key on top of the camera (left), advanced each of the 100 exposures. The 6-inch-long leather carrying case (right), added a portable feature. Thousands were sold for $25 to people who valued its ease of operation. The rarity of these now-historic cameras easily elicits a price of **$1,500** from collectors. *Photos above and below courtesy of Allen and Hilary Weiner, New York City.*

Detective Camera

William Schmid, of Brooklyn, New York, invented the first American hand-held camera, which E. & H.T. Anthony and Company manufactured in 1883. Photographers found this camera miraculously small and easy to operate. Because it allowed the photographer to be less conspicuous, it was dubbed the detective camera. It is valued at **$1,200.**

The Entertainers

The evanescent nature of the performing arts eludes possession. No matter how often one watched Sarah Bernhardt perform, it was impossible to take her home; instead, one tried to preserve a memory with a playbill, poster, or other souvenir of the production.

Theater and Ballet: Today, theatrical memorabilia holds historical and monetary value, even for those who were never among the audience. For example, if someone hadn't saved the playbill, how many people would know that Edgar Allen Poe's mother once played Ophelia (p. 122)? Or that the portrait of a favorite turn-of-the-century actress was available on a pin button, just like a politician's (p. 125)? And sentiment aside, these delightful mementos, some of which were often given away, are now worth hundreds of times their original cost. A program from Diaghilev's *Ballet Russe* is worth more than a pair of box seats (p. 126), and while theaters no longer offer such fabulous souvenirs as crystal slippers (p. 124), it might be wise to treasure the tee shirts that proclaim today's productions.

Movies: Movie star mementos, acquired lovingly over the years, may turn out to have been a good investment of time and money. Local movie house posters the management considered clutter, if saved, could be appreciating today. Photoplay editions of movies, illustrated with stills (p. 128), have been issued by book publishers since the 1920s. These and old movie magazines, especially those featuring Katherine Hepburn from the 1930s, are valuable now (p. 129).

Music: Early recordings by stars as great as Caruso or Nicolai Figner (p. 134) are valuable, but there are also rarities among the lp's and 45's recorded by contemporary pop stars. While you were enjoying Elvis's rendition of "Jingle Bells" on his classic Christmas Album (p. 134), you might have missed a greater reward if the original sheet music for a tune called "One Horse Open Sleigh" slipped through your fingers. Like books, printed music has equally valuable first editions. It is unlikely that you will ever see a first edition of the "Star Spangled Banner" (p. 135); only ten are known to exist. But if your great-grandparents were ragtime fans at the turn of the century, you might find a piano bench full of valuable Scott Joplin tunes (p. 136). Early music machines, from the elegant Edisons (p. 130-131) to the funky portable Mikiphones, that livened up beach parties in the 20s (p. 132), are now as costly as modern stereo components. Undoubtedly, early model television sets will seem as odd to us in 2077 as old graphophones do today.

Suggested Reading:

Frow, George L., comp. *Guide to the Edison Cylinder Phonograph: A Handbook for Collectors*, Antony, 1970.

Fuld, James J. *Book of World-Famous Music: Classical, Folk, and Popular*, rev. ed., Crown, 1971.

Gelatt, Roland. *The Fabulous Phonograph*, Appleton-Century-Crofts, 1966.

Hazelcorn, Howard. *A Collector's Guide to the Columbia Spring-Wound Cylinder Gramophone 1894-1910*. Antique Phonograph Monthly Monograph Series, 1976.

Read, Oliver, and Walter Welch. *From Tin Foil to Stereo*, Howard W. Sams, Inc., 1975.

The Record Collector, Ipswich, Suffolk, Eng.

Theater

Sarah Bernhardt at San Quentin

If you were unfortunate enough to be in San Quentin on Washington's Birthday, 1913, at least you would have seen Sarah Bernhardt perform there in *Une Nuit de Noel sous la Terreur*. Sarah Bernhardt memorabilia is extremely collectible. This photograph of that production is valued at **$75.** *All photos pages 121-125, unless otherwise indicated, courtesy Boothbay Theatre Museum, Franklyn Lenthall-Curator. Photo above: Thom Loughman.*

Maude Adams Figurine

So popular was the actress Maude Adams that Colorado sent a solid gold life-size statue of her to the Paris Exhibition of 1889. It weighed 712 lbs. and was valued at $125,000. This 6-inch gilded china figurine is a replica of that statue. When it was made in 1890, it was given away. Now it is valued at **$100.** *Photo: Thom Loughman.*

Hamlet Playbill

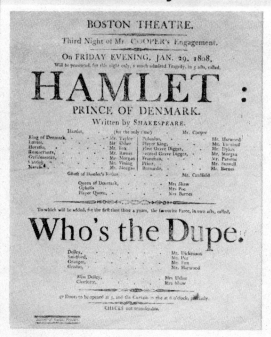

Edgar Allen Poe was not the only member of his family with talent. This playbill shows that his mother played Ophelia in a production of *Hamlet* in Boston, in 1808. This rare playbill could easily cost a collector **$150**. *Photo: Carroll Dinsmore.*

Actress Glass Celery Holder

Actress glass, last made in 1879, is one of the rarest types of pattern glass, imprinted with portraits of stage favorites of the day. This celery holder, with a scene from Gilbert and Sullivan's *H.M.S. Pinafore*, could have been purchased for $20 five years ago. Today a more realistic price would be close to **$60**. *Photo: Thom Loughman.*

Romeo and Juliet Figurine

Charlotte Cushman, America's first great tragic actress, is seen here playing Romeo. Her sister Susan is Juliet. These girls from Boston were great friends of Elizabeth Barrett and Robert Browning. This figurine is rare for two reasons: there are few statues of women playing men's roles, and all theatrical Staffordshire increases in value each year. When this was made it was quite inexpensive. Ten years ago, it could have been purchased for **$25**. Today it would cost at least **$150**. *Photo: Thom Loughman.*

Edwin Booth's Farewell Performance

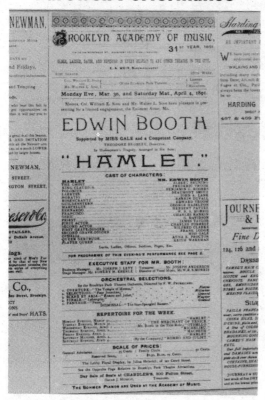

This playbill is from Edwin Booth's last perform- ance of *Hamlet*, given in Brooklyn on April 4, 1891. Booth was a noted Shakespearean actor, and is thought to have been America's greatest Hamlet. This playbill is valued at **$100**. *Photo: Thom Loughman.*

Souvenir Spoon

This spoon was made as a souvenir of the Actors' Fund Fair in 1892. In the bowl of the spoon is a picture of New York's famous Park Theatre. The handle shows five actors on the back and five actresses on the front. Such spoons are worth **$100** today. *Photo: Caroll Dinsmore.*

Theatrical Playing Cards

This pack of playing cards, decorated with a different actor or actress on each card, cost 50¢ at the turn of the century; it is now valued at **$50**. What could be a more de- lightful way to spend an eve- ning than playing cards with Eleanora Duse, Mrs. Patrick Campbell, Otis Skinner, and 50 other celebrities? *From the collection of Dennis Southers.*

Glass Slipper

Would **$50** be a high price for one shoe? Not if you were a collector, and that shoe was the elegant glass slipper given as a souvenir at the play *The Crystal Slipper* in 1891. This 6-inch slipper, engraved on the bottom, would delight any Cinderella, provided she had small feet. *Photo: Carroll Dinsmore.*

Mary Green Dolls

Mary Green was a theater buff and a doll maker. Combining these two interests, she created over 500 dolls representing actors and actresses in roles they created. These dolls have become collectors' items and now cost **$125-200** each. From left to right are Marjorie Rambeau in *Goldfish* (1922), Joseph Stanley in *All Over Town* (1915) and Ina Claire in *Biography* (1932). *The Ballet Shop, New York City.*

Edwin Forrest Girandole

In the mid-1800s, Edwin Forrest was one of America's first great stars. This 14-inch brass figural candelabrum ornamented with glass prisms, called a girandole, shows Forrest in a role he made famous in America and England— *Metamora or The Last of the Wampanoags.* It is valued at **$100.** *Photo: Thom Loughman.*

Rogers Group

John Rogers was a 19th-century American sculptor who created a popular series of 80 small plaster groups illustrating literary, historical, and humorous subjects. These "Rogers Groups" were made from bronze master models, and it is estimated that over 80,000 were sold. This group, showing a scene from Shakespeare's *As You Like It,* was patented in 1881. It is one of Rogers' eleven theater groups, and was sold at auction for **$1,025.** *From a private collection.*

Actress Pin-Buttons

In the 1890s a button maker in New York fell in love with an actress. As a joke, he placed her picture on the pin-buttons. Her friends were so wildly excited about the idea, he made thousands of them with different actresses. They sold originally for 10¢ each. Now they bring up to **$10**, depending on the actress's picture. *Photo: Carroll Dinsmore.*

Stein's Theatrical Face Powder

This tin can of theatrical make-up from the early 1900s would make any theater buff nostalgic. A collector of tin cans, or someone who just loves theater, might pay up to **$50** for it. *From the collection of Mr. and Mrs. Jerry M. Matz.*

Dance

Ballet Theatre Program

The Ballet Theatre was established in 1939 in New York City in an attempt to create a national American ballet company. It has since become known as the American Ballet Theatre, and is respected internationally for its contributions to dance. This souvenir program from its 1953 season sold originally for $1; today it is valued at **$8.** *All items this page courtesy of The Ballet Shop, New York City, and opposite page from Norman Crider's Ballet, Opera, and Theatre Gallery, New York City.*

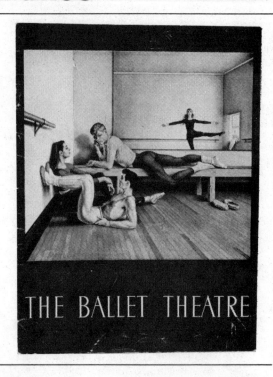

THE BALLET THEATRE

Ballet Russe Program

Serge Diaghilev's Ballet Russe created a revolution in ballet. Diaghilev encouraged experimentation in movement, music, and scenic design, and for the first time in the history of ballet the male dancer was the star and was no longer subordinate to the female star. When *Le Sacré du Printemps* opened in Paris in 1913, Stravinsky's discordant score and Nijinsky's unorthodox choreography created a sensation that almost resulted in a riot. In 1916 the company and Nijinsky made their first American appearance in a tour of the U.S. This program from that tour, containing the Leon Bakst costume designs shown below, left, is valued at **$100.**

Anna Pavlova as The Dying Swan

Anna Pavlova created one of the magical moments in dance history when she took her bow as The Dying Swan. This figurine, made by Rosenthal in 1915, was one of many figurines of entertainers of the day. It is valued at **$450**.

Tango Figurine

This bisque figurine was made in Germany in the 1920s for export to England. It was part of a series made to illustrate popular social dances of the day. The tango became an international sensation in 1921 after Rudolph Valentino danced it in *The Four Horsemen of the Apocalypse*. This couple is valued at **$85.**

Fanny Elssler Basket

This delicate basket was made in France in the 1850s. Inlaid in mother-of-pearl and ivory is a picture of the Austrian-born ballerina Fanny Elssler, who achieved instant popularity when she and her sister danced with the Paris Opera in the 1830s. She often danced pas de deux with her sister Thérèse, who played the male role, establishing the precedent for having the male parts in French ballets danced by women. As an example of a Victorian basket, this would be valued at $50-$60; the picture of Fanny Elssler increases its value to **$165.**

Cigar Case

In France and England between 1830 and 1850, it was fashionable for a gentleman to express adoration for a favorite performer by having her portrait on his cigar case. This particular ballerina cigar case is valued at **$135.**

Movies

Window Card

In the 1920s, window cards, advertising the current feature at the local theater, were displayed by all the neighboring merchants. Because they were made of cardboard, they were intended to have a short period of usefulness, and few of these wonderful works have survived. Those which have are sometimes worth as much as **$100**. *All items pages 128 and 129 courtesy of Cinemabilia, N.Y.C.*

Novelized Movie

Lilac Time, which starred Colleen Moore and Gary Cooper, was such a popular film that Grosset and Dunlap published a novelized version in 1928, filled with pictures from the photoplay, as movies were called in the 1920s. Guy Fowler was the writer who turned screenplay to novel. These novelized versions of films were extremely popular in the 1920s and appeared again during the 1940s. The cover graphics are just part of what makes *Lilac Time* worth **$12** to collectors.

Gone With The Wind Paperback

Gone With The Wind, a popular novel which became an even more popular film, was republished in this paperback motion picture edition by Macmillan in 1940. With pictures of Clark Gable and Vivian Leigh, the book makes the film live on, and fans will pay **$13** for this collectible novel.

Screen Romances Magazine

Screen Romances is the most sought after of all the movie magazines. This August, 1933 issue, which sports Katherine Hepburn on the cover, is worth **$25.** The magazine consisted of credits and synopses of all the latest movies, as well as stills which gave readers a preview of the action.

Photoplay Magazine

When James R. Quirk edited *Photoplay* in the 1930s, it was the most prestigious of American movie publications. This April, 1930 issue in mint condition brings **$25.** Earl Christy, who did the cover drawing of Norma Shearer, is a collectible artist in his own right.

Phonographs

1900 Edison "Home" Phonograph

This custom, nickel-plated Edison "Home" phonograph in a gilt-decorated cabinet belonged to either a wealthy family or a grand hotel in 1900. The famous Edison signature appears on a metal plate riveted to the machine. The phonograph played two-minute cylinders which, when not in use, were stored within the cabinet. This unique machine is valued at **$4,500** today. *All phonographs pages 130-132 from the collection of Howard Hazelcorn.*

The Maroon Gem

This 1909 Edison Model D was called the Maroon Gem, because its body and horn were painted a beautiful, deep-red color. The phonograph had a small spring-wound motor, and its reproducer was equipped with two styluses so that it played both two- and four-minute cylinders. A gold decal, like the one shown on this oak cabinet, appeared on all of Edison's machines after 1905, as well as Edison's decaled signature, which is not visible here. This phonograph originally sold for $14; its limited production has increased its value to **$575.**

1901 Columbia Graphophone

Bettini Wax Cylinders

This 1901 Columbia Graphophone, also called The Macdonald after the head engineer at Columbia who invented it, is uniquely designed to play five-inch cylinders as well as standard two-inch records. Five-inch brown wax cylinders, like the one shown on the phonograph, reproduced louder and clearer sound than the smaller records, but they were bulky, fragile, and expensive. Because the production of five-inch cylinders was short-lived, Columbia made only a limited number of these phonographs, which originally sold in ornate cases for $25. Now, collectors will pay **$1,200** and up for one.

Bettini meant quality in the turn-of-the-century recording business. Their wax recording cylinders sold for a high $6 each in 1899 and are scarce today. This one, in its original box, was recorded in Paris and is valued at **$300**. Bettini utilized a custom-built recording and reproducing system, which attracted serious music artists as well as prominent social figures to record in his fine studio.

1911 Edison "Home" Phonograph

There were large numbers of this well-made "Home" phonograph produced, and collectors avidly buy them now at **$450**. The metal cygnet horn with attractive wood-grain finish is relatively large and one of Edison's last outside horns. Beginning in 1913, horns were concealed inside the cabinet.

The Mikiphone

A favorite with beachcombers in the 1920s, this portable phonograph, the Mikiphone, sold for $5 and looked like a big pocket watch when enclosed in its 6-inch case. Its spring is wound with the key at the top. Opened and assembled, it becomes a full-fledged music machine, complete with amplifying horn. A collector's prize at **$175.**

Columbia Graphophone

In its competition with the Edison Co. at the turn of the century, the Columbia Phonograph Co. stressed advertising, frequent design changes, and a cheaper product. In 1898, this Graphophone was the cheapest cylinder phonograph on the market, selling for $5 without its oak case. If your grandparents saved one, it is a **$200** treasure now.

Records

Beatles Album

This original cover of The Beatles' album *Yesterday, Today, and Tomorrow* was thought to be offensive; a new cover was designed for the album and was pasted over the picture on those albums already printed. Sensibilities change with the times, however, and Capitol Records now plans to re-release the album with the original cover. An original album with this picture is today valued at **$100-$150.** *Courtesy of Elizabeth Henley, New York City.*

I Only Have Eyes For You

The Swallows was a popular rhythm and blues vocal group in the 1950s. Their version of *I Only Have Eyes For You* sold well, and a second pressing was made. If you're lucky enough to have a record from the first pressing, you have a piece of plastic worth **$100.** Records from the second pressing sell today for **$5** and have the words "High Fidelity" on the label. *Courtesy of Farfel's Records, New York City.*

Damn Yankees

When *Damn Yankees* opened on Broadway on May 5, 1955, it received rave reviews but did poorly at the box office. In a successful attempt to increase attendance, a new advertising campaign was created, stressing the sexier aspects of the show, and playing down its baseball theme. A new record cover was released, replacing the original which pictured Gwen Verdon throwing a baseball. Both albums are out of print, but the selling price for the original starts at **$20,** while the replacement cover starts at **$15.** *Courtesy of Farfel's Records, New York City.*

Elvis Presley's Christmas Album

Elvis Presley recorded this Christmas album for RCA Victor in 1957. It is one of his rarest albums because it was re-issued without the color photographs of Elvis included inside. Today it would cost you **$60** to have this Elvis under your Christmas tree. *Courtesy of Farfel's Records, New York City.*

Louis Armstrong Recording

In Chicago, on February 23, 1926, the blues singer Baby Mack recorded "You've Got to Get Home on Time/What Kind of a Man is That" for Okeh records. She was accompanied on piano by Richard M. Jones and on trumpet by Louis Armstrong, whose jazz improvisations eventually won him world fame. Of all Armstrong's 1920s accompaniments, this Okeh 8313-B recording is considered the rarest. A copy in mint-to-excellent condition would be valued at approximately **$150.** In the case of all rare jazz labels, the condition of the label itself is as important as the condition of the grooves. *Photo courtesy of Institute of Jazz Studies, Rutgers University, Newark, New Jersey.*

Russian Record

Nicolai Figner made this recording of *Pagliacci* in 1900. A popular Russian tenor, he was Tchaikovsky's favorite singer. This record is rare, as many copies of it were destroyed after the 1917 Revolution by owners who were afraid of government retaliation for possessing a czarist record. This collector's item is valued at **$300-$400.** *From the collection of Martin Sokol, New York City.*

Caruso Record

This priceless recording of Enrico Caruso singing *Luna Fedel* was made in 1903. It is one of his earliest and rarest records. There are only five known copies of this record in existence: two of them belong to institutions and cannot be sold, while the other three belong to private collections and are not for sale. *From the collection of Martin Sokol, New York City.*

Sheet Music

The Star Spangled Banner

Francis Scott Key wrote a poem, *The Star Spangled Banner,* to celebrate America's victory over the British at Fort McHenry in 1814. Key was aboard a ship the night of September 13-14, securing the release of a friend under a flag of truce. From the ship, he was able to see the English attack of the fort. As long as the attack continued, it was proof that the fort had not surrendered. When the firing ceased, it was not known whether the fort had surrendered, or if the attack had been abandoned. When the dawn came and Key saw that "our flag was still there," he was inspired to write the poem that was later set to music. It was declared our national anthem by an act of Congress on March 3, 1931. The Smithsonian Institution now has the shellholed flag that Key saw flying over Fort McHenry. This sheet music dates from 1814 and is the first printing of the words and music together. It is valued at **$25,000.** (Notice the misprint of the word patriotic.) *All sheet music pages 135-137 from the collection of James J. Fuld.*

Euphonic Sounds

Scott Joplin was a popular composer at the turn of the century. He is best known for his ragtime music, although he also wrote an opera, *Treemonisha*. The popularity of Joplin's tune, *The Entertainer,* used as the theme of the movie, *The Sting,* has generated new interest in Joplin's work. *Euphonic Sounds,* with a portrait photo of Joplin on the cover, was published in 1909, and is valued at **$75.**

Alexander's Ragtime Band

Alexander's Ragtime Band was written by Irving Berlin in 1911. While the song is not real ragtime, there was a real Alexander—the title referred to a cornet-playing bandleader named Jack Alexander. This first-edition sheet music is valued at **$25.**

Ol' Man River

Showboat opened on Broadway on December 27, 1927, and was an immediate success. It has been performed internationally, been made into a movie twice, and has had many of its songs become standards. The original lyrics of *Ol' Man River* contained references that were offensive to some and have since been modified. This sheet music, published prior to the show's opening, is valued at **$50.** *Ol' Man River,* from the musical production, *Showboat;* Music by Jerome Kern; Lyrics by Oscar Hammerstein II. Copyright © 1927 T.B. Harms Company. Copyright renewed. Used by permission.

I Wish I Was in Dixie

Daniel Emmett, a prominent 19th-century minstrel, wrote the song variously known as *I Wish I Was in Dixie, Dixie's Land,* and *Dixie.* The first authorized edition of *Dixie* was published in June, 1860. A copy of this edition is now valued at **$400.** The sheet music shown is an unauthorized edition made earlier in 1860. Emmett's name does not appear on the cover. There are only three known copies of this printing and each is valued at **$1,000.**

Porgy and Bess

George Gershwin's first attempt at an all-black opera resulted in an unsuccessful one-act, *135th Street,* performed in the stage revue *George White's Scandals of 1923.* With *Porgy and Bess,* however, he wrote what is probably the most successful American opera. This first edition of the piano vocal score, with a portrait of Gershwin, was published Sept. 28, 1935, and is valued at **$50.** *Used with permission of the publisher, Chappell & Co. Inc.*

One Horse Open Sleigh

One Horse Open Sleigh, or *Jingle Bells,* as it is now known, was first published in 1857. It is said to have been written originally as a Sunday-school entertainment. This original sheet music is valued today at **$150.**

Playthings

A toy can inspire nostalgic daydreams, even when the paint is chipped away or it has fallen apart. Collectors who seek the survivors of someone else's playtime often have mixed motivations, for there can be money in those childhood memories.

Tin and Cast Iron Toys: When new, most tin and iron toys, even the best by such famous manufacturers as Ives and George Brown, cost only a few pennies. Today, less than a century later, these appealing creations are skyrocketing in price. A tin camel on wheels (opposite) costs as much as an airflight to Cairo. A complete cast-iron train (p. 141) commands several hundred dollars, and you still have to pull it yourself. Banks are another cast-iron rage. The mechanicals, activated by the drop of a coin, are even more popular than still banks. The Tammany bank (p. 142) snatches a child's pennies without a scruple. Coins turn the globe of the Atlas bank, which turns collectors' heads at $1,700.

Parlor Games: Adults, too, have had their diversions. Card games are an old and sometimes lucrative amusement. But with cards from czarist Russia (p. 145), any hand is worth money, since the deck is valued at over $100. More unusual pastimes include optical games, like the psychedelic Magic Mirror and carpet balls (p. 147), which transformed the outdoor French sport *Boule* into an indoor game.

Characters and Comics: Premiums from the great serials are far from free now; your Little Orphan Annie "Shake-Up" Mug (p. 150) may be a $25 treasure. When the radio was off, the fantastic comic book superheroes absorbed your attention. English teachers may have bemoaned your interest, but bankers would praise your investment. Certain issues now bring four-figure sums (pp. 152-53).

Baseball Memorabilia: Trading baseball cards was more popular than trading comic books. After all, you could "flip" baseball cards. Hundreds of pink gum slabs were chewed to obtain a year's cards. Now, if you want a hard-to-find Jackie Robinson from the 1952 series (p. 156), it will take a cool $20.

Dolls: There are probably more doll collectors than enthusiasts for all other toys and games combined. Competition to find the best dolls is intense. The beautiful face of a Tête Jumeau (p. 157) is easy to fall in love with, but as Tiny Grimes once sang, "Romance without finance is a nuisance"—it takes $800 to buy this sweetheart. Less costly, but no less endearing, are Teddy Bears (p. 160), who have also joined the price war.

Miniatures: Miniatures delight those who find beauty in smallness, and for those who have preserved such treasures, the rewards can be enormous. A miniature desk (p. 165) can be just as expensive as its full-sized prototype. A 3-inch Lynnfield sideboard (p. 163) in the Art Deco style costs slightly less than one white truffle. If you can't afford to furnish two homes, will you choose elegance on a doll's scale or your own?

Suggested Reading:

Bellows, Ina H. *Old Mechanical Banks*. Lightner, 1954.

Coleman, Dorothy S. et al. *Collector's Encyclopedia of Dolls*. Crown, 1968.

Hertz, Louis, *The Toy Collector*. Funk and Wagnall's, 1969.

Hochman, Gene. *Encyclopedia of American Playing Cards*, part I. 29 Hampton Terrace, Livingston, N.J. 07039, 1976.

Horn, Maurice, Ed. *The World Encyclopedia of Comics*. Chelsea House, 1976.

Jacobs, Flora Gill. *A History of Doll Houses*, Charles Scribner's Sons, 1976.

Meyer, John D., and L. Freeman. *Old Penny Banks: Mechanical, Still*. Century, 1960.

Overstreet, Bob. *The Comic Book Price Guide*. Harmony, 1976.

Pressland, David. *The Art of the Tin Toy*. Crown, 1976.

Sugar, Bert. *The Sports Collector's Bible*. Wallace-Homestead, 1975.

Tin and Cast-Iron Toys

Studebaker Pedal Car

This 1925 Studebaker, 4½ feet long, is all metal with a ritzy radiator cap. The running board becomes a makeshift luggage carrier when the lattice gate is stretched across. In back, the license plate flips up when the brake is pulled to flash "STOP" at the driver behind. The turn of a crank simulates the sound of a real motor. This toy was never inexpensive; and collectors will pay as much as **$700** for it today.

Camel on Wheels

The eccentric wheels on this 19th-century tin pull toy insure a suitably camellike gait. And, of course, the bell on his back rings with every bump. Would the imperturbable camel driver blink if he knew the auction price of **$580**?

Marx Merrymakers

Wind them up and they rap a neat beat. Don't you wish you'd saved your tin mouse band, especially because one might sell for more than **$150** today? These American toys from the 1930s were also manufactured for a time in England, giving collectors on both sides of the Atlantic a chance at making a delightful discovery.

Tin Water Carrier

George Brown is a magic name to toy collectors. His designs for inexpensive tin toys, such as the water carrier shown here, brought him fame in the 1870s and '80s. This and other designs can be authenticated in *The George Brown Sketchbook,* published by Pyne Press, Princeton, New Jersey. Any Brown toy in excellent condition is worth at least **$450.**

Cast-Iron Train

When this Ives train was made in the 1890s, it sold for very little. A complete set included locomotive, tender, and three freight cars, each approximately 8 inches long. This one, with three of its original parts, is now a **$300-400** toy. It would cost more, of course, with all its cars. Most cast iron is not marked, but pieces can be authenticated through old Ives catalogs.

Cast-Iron Pumper

Fire toys were as popular in 1910 as they are today. Collectors treasure those made by Hubley or Kenton, but not all are marked. The cast-iron pumper shown here is one of the most desirable fire toys, easily worth **$275** or more in good condition.

Hansom Cab

This very rare pull toy is hard to find with all of its three parts — cab, driver, and horse — intact. This one, painted black with yellow wheels, was made by Pratt and Letchworth of Buffalo, N.Y., circa 1910. It stands about 6 inches high and could command **$750.**

Banks

The Tammany

Girl in Victorian Chair

This is Boss Tweed, infamous Tammany Hall leader, comfortably ensconced in his chair and waiting to take your money. It seems appropriate that such a figure should have inspired this first mechanical bank, made in the 1870s. When a penny is inserted in Boss Tweed's right hand between thumb and fingers, the right arm rotates down to meet the left hand, where the coin drops into a slot. Appearing to have tucked the coin in his coat, Boss Tweed nods in silent affirmation of his personal gain. This bank is quite common but beware of reproductions. Originals bear the lattice work evident at the back and sides of his chair and, if in mint condition like this, should bring **$125-$300.**

This little girl, curled in a Victorian chair with a puppy in her lap, seems innocent of her attractiveness. In 1976, this cast-iron bank, missing much paint, brought **$1,900** at auction. *Photo courtesy of PB84, a division of Sotheby Parke Bernet, Inc., New York City.*

Indian and Bear Bank

The cast-iron bank shown here, made around 1910, is particularly intricate. When a penny is deposited in the rifle, the Indian shoots it at the bear. The bear's belly stores the savings. An unusual notion, the bank brought **$325** at auction.

Eagle and Eaglets Bank

The tasty morsel of a penny, when loaded into this mother bird's beak, ignites a mechanical spectacle. The mother flaps her wings as she drops the coin into the nest of eaglets, who open wide and chirp with ravenous joy. This heartwarming cast-iron bank drew a **$275** bid at an auction in 1975. *Photo courtesy of PB84, a division of Sotheby Parke Bernet, Inc., New York City.*

Atlas Bank

"Money moves the world" is the hard-nosed message embossed on this mechanical bank. When a coin is inserted and the lever pressed, the paper-covered globe spins around. This Atlas's burden is in perfect condition. Rarity, however, is the major factor in determining a mechanical bank's value. A collector paid **$1,700** for this bank at an auction in 1976. *Courtesy of PB84, a division of Sotheby Parke Bernet, Inc., New York City.*

Parlor Games

Joan of Arc Transformation Deck

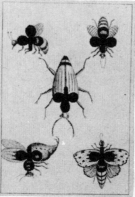

This deck is one of a series of six transformation decks produced from 1805 to 1811 by J. G. Cotta of Tubingen, Germany, which range in price from **$400** to **$600**. A transformation deck is one in which the pips of every spot card are integrated into the design drawn on the card. Joan of Arc, the deck's namesake, and other figures — characters from Schiller's *Joan of Arc* — play the roles of king, queen, and jack, but the collector is more interested in the humorous transformation designs which fill each numerical card. *All items pages 144-146 from the collection of Gene Hochman.*

Grammar Cards

Decks made before the French Revolution had the traditional figures of king, queen, and jack on the face cards, as seen in this Parisian example from 1770. During the Revolution, these decks of playing cards were confiscated and distributed to schools, which used their empty backs as educational "flash cards." Here, the overturned cards reveal French verb endings; this "school material" is worth **$100.**

American Transformation Deck

This clever transformation deck, designed by C.E. Carryl in 1879, was an advertising device of the prestigious New York jeweler, Tiffany and Company. It was probably sent out as a gift to the store's customers; now it commands **$125.** The integration of the pips into pictures never ceases to be a source of visual enjoyment; here, for example, spades are the torsos of three men seen in profile, while the hearts make interesting bloomers.

Russian Playing Cards

Decks of cards from czarist Russia are quite rare and, depending on their condition, range from **$100** to **$300** in value. The figures of royalty drawn on these 1867 cards are embellished with gilt.

French Revolution Deck

During the French Revolution, nobility was in disfavor, and decks of cards were altered accordingly. The new heroes of society were senators, like Brutus, and philosophers, like Rousseau. This deck of cards, designed by Minot in 1792, utilized dots to indicate the ranks of the three face cards: the single dot stood for the equivalent of kings; two dots represented a queen. This deck brings **$350** today.

The Rump Parliament Deck

Oliver Cromwell's Rump Parliament is the subject of biting satire in the 52 pictures which form this historic deck, printed around 1684. Because of its disrespectful nature, it was probably not produced in England, but in Holland, where the exiled monarch Charles II had received a sympathetic welcome. These anti-Cromwell cards are a **$750** collector's item now.

The Seminole Wars Deck

Published by J. Y. Humphrey's of Philadelphia in 1819, the face cards in this deck commemorate America's early wars with the Seminole Indians. The four kings are American presidents; pictured at right is Andrew Jackson. The Indian chiefs play the role of jacks, as shown on the center card. Since few heroines were recognized during this period, the queen figures took on allegorical roles: Blind Justice favors one side with riches here. The deck is valued at **$500.**

The Compendium of Geography

This deck of English cards, printed in 1780, is called *The Compendium of Geography*. The pips cover a small space in the upper left-hand corner, while the rest of each card is devoted to information about the geography of the four continents, one of which is described throughout each suit. The cards shown here act as aces in the deck, but the rest of the pips are numbered. There are only 25 to 30 known copies of this deck, worth **$350** each.

Praxinoscope

This pre-cinema toy, known as a praxinoscope, was made in France in 1878. Today it is an expensive plaything, commanding roughly **$450**. Measuring about 4 inches high, the praxinoscope is constructed so that a strip of pictures, placed inside the drum, is reflected on the mirrors at the center. When the drum is spun, the pictures form a moving picture of a woman batting a shuttlecock. *Courtesy of Allen and Hilary Weiner, New York City.*

Optical Toy

The Magic Mirror, an anamorphic toy, consists of a reflecting tube and hand-tinted lithographs distorted beyond recognition. The mirrorlike curved surface of the tube resolves the flat image on paper into a readable form. Here, the reflection reveals a Roman soldier in the mysterious paper. In the 1890s, adults played with this optical device made by McLaughlin Brothers of New York. The game, now worth **$250,** still makes marvelous, if expensive, entertainment. *Courtesy of Allen and Hilary Weiner, New York City.*

Glass Swirls

Antique glass marbles with colorful center swirls are highly prized by collectors. Pontil marks — rough areas where the marble was cut from the glassblower's rod — should be evident where the colors converge. The swirls, over 2 inches in diameter, sell for as much as **$40.** *From the collection of Hilary Cochran.*

Staffordshire Carpet Balls

One must imagine that Victorian ladies did indeed restrain themselves when rolling these grapefruit-sized, ceramic carpet balls across the carpet floor. Otherwise, none would have remained unbroken and collectible at **$50-$60** each.

Characters and Comics

Minnie Mouse Doll

This Steiff Minnie Mouse doll, made in 1936, is quite rare. Many dolls have been made of Mickey Mouse, but few of Minnie. She stands about 12 inches high, wears a felt skirt, is stuffed, and sold originally for $7.50. Today she is valued around **$300.** *All photos this page and opposite courtesy of Old Friends, New York City.*

Pinocchio Figures

These bisque figurines of the characters in the cartoon *Pinocchio* (from left to right: Figaro, Jiminy Cricket, Gepetto, Pinocchio, and The Fox) originally sold for a nickel or less at Woolworth's. Today they cost from **$18** to **$20** each.

Mickey Mouse Watch

The term "Mickey Mouse Watch" is commonly used today to mean a cheap watch. In 1933, when Macy's sold 11,000 Mickey Mouse watches in one day at $1.95 each, this may have been true, but no longer. Today, one of those same watches without its original box, in working condition and with a strap, could bring up to **$200**. With its original box and original strap, and in mint condition, its value may be increased to **$300**.

Donald Duck Toy

Goofy and Pluto are among the friends that surrounded Donald Duck on this celluloid pull-toy from the 1930s. Because all the Disney characters that had been created are represented on this extremely flammable and perishable toy, it is valued between **$350** and **$400**.

Mickey Mouse Book

In 1928 Walt Disney made *Steamboat Willey*, the first animated sound cartoon, featuring Mickey Mouse, a character that has since become world famous. Mickey was featured on every possible sort of promotional item: cartoons, comic books, books, and toys. Mickey is even printed on T-shirts made today, although his image has been somewhat altered from the original Disney design. This Mickey Mouse book, published by McKay in 1931, has a green cloth binding with a paper cover pasted on, and is valued at **$50** today.

Little Orphan Annie Premiums

The adventures of Little Orphan Annie were told in serial form on the radio in the '30s. A secret message given at the end of each show could be deciphered by sending away for the metal decoder pictured at top. Nostalgia buffs now pay up to **$15** for it. Ovaltine, the show's sponsor, also offered a premium – a Bakelite shake-up mug offered in exchange for two Ovaltine box tops and a dime. The mug is now worth as much as **$30.** *Premium from the collection of Foster B. Pollack; shake-up mug courtesy of Flemington Doll and Toy Museum, Flemington, N.J.*

Blondie's Jalopy

Blondie was a popular comic strip in the '30s when this wind-up, tin toy was manufactured. This model exaggerates the sleek lines of the cars of the period and shows other characters from the comic strip. Jalopy is the right description, for these toys usually fell apart after several crashes against the living room wall. Relative scarcity makes them worth **$250.** *Courtesy of Flemington Doll and Toy Museum.*

Harold Lloyd Bell

Most character toys would pale next to this 5-inch-high bicycle bell featuring the face of the great silent film comedian Harold Lloyd. Stamped from tin and lithographed, it's a face that's worth at least **$100.** *Courtesy of Speakeasy, New York City.*

Barney Google and Spark Plug

The comic strip team of Barney Google and his trusty horse Spark Plug, were two of the many cartoon characters reproduced in toy form for children in the '20s. Their jointed wooden bodies kept them dancing all the time, much to the delight of the children who played with them. Now adults thrill to their antics and collect them for **$100** each. *Courtesy of Flemington Doll and Toy Museum.*

Betty Boop

Max Fleisher's animated creation Betty Boop was one of the most popular female film stars of the 1930s. Manufacturers were only too glad to sell Betty Boop dolls for a dollar. Today, an 8-inch doll like this one goes for as much as **$200.** *Courtesy of Flemington Doll and Toy Museum.*

Beatles Cel

Thousands of pictures hand painted on clear celluloid are used in the creation of one animated film, such as *Yellow Submarine.* This cel of John Lennon from that film is a rare piece of Beatlemania at **$40-$60.** *Courtesy of Speakeasy, New York City.*

Nixon-Agnew Puppets

Lots of these spirited rubber hand puppets, designed by Rick Meyerowitz, were sold for $8.95 through an ad in the *National Lampoon* in 1968. While they can still be found for as little as **$10** a pair, they might not be so available in 10 or 15 years. *Courtesy of Speakeasy.*

Detective Comics

In this issue of Detective Comics, Batman, that mysterious and avenging creature of the night, made his debut. Later, Batman had his own series of comics. This first featured appearance predates even the existence of Robin. The hero soared to fame in movies and television, as well as in comics. A good copy of this book would cost a collector a fancy price — in the neighborhood of **$3,000.** *All photos this page and opposite courtesy of Phil Seuling, Brooklyn, New York.*

Four Color Comics Number 9

Each book in Dell's Four Color comics series had a different title and featured different characters from comic strip material. Published in 1942, Number 9, shown here, contains the early work of Disney's best-known artist, Carl Barks, whose Donald Duck and Uncle Scrooge stories are highly prized. A copy of this book in excellent condition would bring **$1,000**.

Action Comics Number 1

The original costumed superhero was Superman, who made his first appearance in this comic book published by DC comics in 1938. Within two years, imitators had created hundreds of costumed, caped, and masked figures. The price of this Action Number 1, however — about **$5,000** — bears witness to the respect that Superman commands as the father of the comic-book heroes.

Red Raven Number 1

A second issue of Red Raven Comics was never published, but stronger and longer-lasting titles sprang from this experiment of the Marvel Publishing Company. Books by this publisher are constantly sought by collectors. If the lucky owner of Red Raven Number 1 were to ask **$800** for this Marvel, the price would not meet strong resistance from serious collectors.

Marvel Comics Number 1

After publication of the first issue, the title of this series was changed to the more familiar Marvel Mystery Comics. An early entry in the superhero derby, it introduced such characters as The Human Torch and Submariner, figures destined for long lives in the comics. Relatively few copies of the issue shown at left were printed. Because, in addition to being scarce, the book contains the work of famous artists and is the first of a valuable series, copies command top prices. They have sold for more than **$6,000** in the past, and would certainly exceed that figure now.

Baseball Memorabilia

Autographed Baseball

Someone took this baseball to a New York Yankees game in 1951 and got the whole team to sign it. 1951 was the only year that Joe DiMaggio and Mickey Mantle played together, and the signatures of these two superstars up the value of this ball to **$100**. *All items pages 154-156 from the collection of Shelly Goorfin.*

Baseball Advertising

In 1952, a cardboard announcement like this reared its colorful head from every six-pack of Coke. Ten different players were featured in the advertising campaign, and of course kids wanted to collect the whole set. No doubt the idea helped sell cartons of Coke and tickets to the games of the New York area teams. The kids profited, too, by studying the free professional pointers on the back of each card. If the complete set of 10 was saved, it brings a second windfall of **$300** today.

Joe DiMaggio Baseball Card

This very early card, featuring Joe DiMaggio, was produced by Gum, Inc., in 1939. What was once a premium now costs **$10**.

Yogi Berra Baseball Card

LARRY BERRA
Outfield, New York, A.L.

"Walk" today to your food store and buy TIP-TOP

Look for the stars on the TIP-TOP wrapper and the stars on the diamond.

Enriched
TIP-TOP is Better Bread.

There are 15 photos of your favorite baseball players in this club group. Should you get duplicate photos (two or more of same player) trade cards until you have the complete set.
Root for your home team and for **TIP-TOP BREAD.**
Compliments of TIP-TOP Bakers

What a thrill it must have been to get a baseball card without having to invest in a stick of gum! Stacks of Tip-Top Bread cards sat on the counters at the local grocery, free for the taking as often as a kid's collector's heart desired. There were 165 cards in the 1947 edition—15 cards for each of the 11 featured teams. Without vital statistics on the backs, they may have seemed less valuable than others to a child concerned with batting averages, but Tip-Top Bread cards are worth **$40** now.

Baseball Autographs

Almost every juvenile baseball fan at some point gets brave enough to hang around after the game asking for autographs. If your team has won, the players are more than happy to spend time outside the locker room, creating future treasures. These autographs, of Mickey Mantle, Rogers Hornsby, and Cy Young, are worth up to **$25** each.

Honus Wagner Baseball Card

As far as baseball cards go, Honus Wagner has become a legend. A non-smoker, Wagner was angered when tobacco companies started putting his picture on their premium cards. Fearing that the proximity of the tobacco to the cards would tempt youngsters to play with both, Wagner had all the remaining stock of tobacco cards which pictured him destroyed. Sometimes, however, one turns up, and collectors pay **$1,000** and up to get it. The card pictured here, which advertises nothing more harmful than cocoa, is a mere **$5,** even though it was one of the earliest, published in 1910.

Jackie Robinson Baseball Card

Topps has meant baseball cards to every bubble-gum-chewing baseball fan since 1951, when the company first began producing them. Topps issues several series of cards per year; in 1952, their series #311-407 was produced in relatively small quantities. This 1952 Jackie Robinson card #312 is thus a rarity. The fact that he was the first black major league player also contributes to this card's **$20** value.

Dolls

Tête Jumeau

This beautiful, blue-eyed bisque-head doll was manufactured by the prestigious French family Jumeau, who produced their famous dolls from 1842 to 1899. The back of the head is marked "Tête Jumeau." This is one of several marks that were used to identify Jumeau dolls during different periods. The blonde wig is of human hair; the jointed wooden body shows signs of repainting. Even so, and without costume, the doll sold for **$800** at auction. *Photo courtesy of PB84, a division of Sotheby Parke Bernet, Inc., New York City.*

French Fashion Doll

In the 19th century French couturiers sent these dolls to American women of wealth to show the fashions of the coming season. They were never intended as toys. This elegant lady wears the original gown she had when made in 1860. She is valued at **$2,000.** *Courtesy of Raggedy Ann Antique Doll and Toy Museum, Flemington, N.J.*

Bisque-Head Doll

This Armand Marseille doll was made in Germany around 1910. The head is made of bisque and the body of wood. This doll is unusual because it has an Irish face (most dolls made in Germany have German faces). This Irish lass is valued at **$265.** *Courtesy of Antique Dolls by Iris Brown, New York City.*

Minerva Doll

Minerva became a registered trademark for this doll in 1894. Marked with a plumed helmet, she has a tin head, molded hair, painted features, a kid body, and bisque hands. When originally made she cost less than $10. Today she costs nearly **$125.** *Courtesy of Antique Dolls by Iris Brown, New York City.*

Frozen Charlotte Doll

Schoenhut Doll

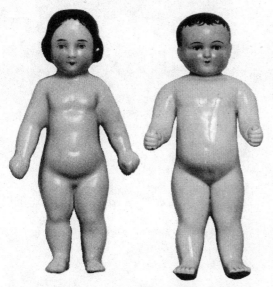

Badenkinder (bathing baby) was the official name of this doll, made around 1850. It was also known as the pillar or stick doll because of its immobile limbs but it was most widely known as the Frozen Charlotte doll, named after a popular ballad of the day. In the song a young girl named Charlotte goes to a dance without a coat in an open sleigh. On arriving at the dance, it is discovered that poor Charlotte has frozen to death. The little Charlotte shown here is unique because of the "pink luster" flesh tone and is valued at **$125**. Her friend Frozen Charlie is valued at **$375**. *All items this page courtesy of Raggedy Ann Antique Doll and Toy Museum.*

Albert Schoenhut patented his doll design in 1911, in Philadelphia. His product became known as the "unbreakable doll" and was popular because of its construction. It was made of wood with a steel spring. The band around the short, boyish hair is a seldom seen feature and adds to this model's uniqueness. This doll is valued at **$375**.

Palmer Cox's Brownie

In the late 1800s, Palmer Cox's Brownies took America by storm. Cox designed twelve different variations of these elfin creatures which were made into rag dolls, including an Indian, a policeman, an Irishman, and a dude (made at the request of Theodore Roosevelt). This typical Brownie, marked with an 1892 copyright on his right foot, is valued at **$50**.

Teddy Bear

In 1902, when Theodore Roosevelt went to Mississippi to settle a boundary dispute, he took a few days off to go bear hunting. The presidential party failed to find any game except for a frightened bear cub, and Teddy Roosevelt refused to shoot the defenseless creature. A political cartoon in *The Washington Post* showed the president turning away from the trembling cub with one hand raised and the other holding a gun. The cartoon, reprinted in newspapers across the country, captured the imagination of the nation. A letter was sent to the White House requesting permission to use the president's name on a series of toy bears, and so began the craze of the Teddy Bear. Bears made prior to 1906 had a hump on the back to make the toys look more lifelike, which increases their current value. This bear, made in 1902, is valued at **$125.** *Courtesy of Raggedy Ann Antique Doll and Toy Museum, Flemington, N.J.*

Porcupine Family

The famous Steiff Toy Co. made this family of porcupines in Germany in 1910. The original labels and name tags are intact and increase their value. Micki, Mecki, Mucki, and Macki, as they are named, would sell today for **$220.** *Antique Dolls by Iris Brown, New York City.*

Campbell Kids

Soup's on! Any mother who has served her family Campbell's Soup is familiar with the faces of the Campbell kids. These are the originals, dated 1910, and are valued at **$250.** *Courtesy of Raggedy Ann Antique Doll and Toy Museum.*

French Mechanical Doll

A twist of a key sets this charming French mechanical doll in motion. Made in 1878 by Jumeau, she seems to knit when the mechanism is activated. She is valued at **$2,500**. *All items this page courtesy of Raggedy Ann Antique Doll and Toy Museum.*

Swimming Doll

This unique doll actually swims. She is made of cork, and her arms and legs move in a swimming motion by means of a clock mechanism inside her. Made in 1878, she wears her original bathing suit. To watch her frolic in the water today, you would have to pay **$350**.

Party Favor Doll

This lovely doll, created by Jumeau in 1844, was made to be broken. French aristocrats gave such dolls to guests, who smashed them, as a grand gesture, at the end of a party. Those that escaped this sad fate are valued at **$500** today.

Kewpie Dolls

In 1913, Rose O'Neill created the kewpie doll. It was so popular that kewpie clothes, games, and books soon followed. The kewpie doll is so revered in Missouri, where Rose O'Neill spent much of her life, that there is an annual celebration in her honor, called the "kewpiesta." One of the most popular dolls among collectors today, the kewpie originally sold for less than $1. Today this white bisque kewpie sells for up to **$125.** The black composition kewpie is quite rare (it was not until recently that black dolls were produced in quantity) and is priced at **$65.** *Raggedy Ann Doll and Toy Museum.*

Two-Faced Doll

This doll's remarkably lifelike frown changes to a dimpled smile when the bisque head is rotated. She stands 13½ inches high and is marked "C.B.," which probably stands for Carl Bergner, a doll manufacturer around the turn of the century who obtained patents for multi-faced dolls. In full costume and in perfect condition, she sold at auction for **$625.** *Photo courtesy of PB84, a division of Sotheby Parke Bernet, Inc., New York City.*

Bye-Lo Doll or "Million Dollar Baby"

This charming doll, patented in 1922 by an American woman, Grace Putnam, and distributed all over Europe, was modeled after a three-day-old baby. The first year the doll was on the market sales totalled over a million, and it became known as the "Million Dollar Baby." It has a bisque head and cloth body and originally wholesaled for $30 per dozen. Bye-Lo Babies, named by their designer, now sell for **$275** and up. *Courtesy of Antique Dolls by Iris Brown, New York City.*

Miniatures

Tynietoy Table

From 1924 to 1950, a line of dollhouses and miniature wooden furniture was manufactured by two enterprising women from Providence, Rhode Island. These pieces are fairly simple, and the name "Tynietoy" is branded on the wood. Sets of furniture for entire rooms originally cost $6 to $21 and there was little change in price through the 1950s. In 1976, PB84, a branch of New York's Sotheby Parke Bernet, sold a box of Tynietoy furniture for **$950**. This little butterfly table, which is unusually detailed, is considered very rare; it could bring **$50** to **$100** by itself. *Photos this page courtesy of Milne Miniatures, Robert S. Milne, New York City.*

Lynnfield Miniature

This 3-inch-high, maple wood dining room sideboard was designed and built in the 1930s by a family in Lynnfield, Massachusetts, now famous for their exquisite miniatures. Well-scaled (1 inch = 1 foot) and beautifully constructed, this was part of a complete Art Deco dining room suite which fine department stores sold as toys. The open shelves with rounded corners are typical of Art Deco design. Collectors are now willing to pay **$50** for this Lynnfield piece.

Cast-Iron Cradle

American manufacturers of cast-iron toys also made miniature dollhouse furniture, such as rockers and this lacy painted cradle. Research dates this at circa 1872, giving it an antique value of about **$85.** *Courtesy of Milne Miniatures, Robert S. Milne, New York City.*

Staffordshire Dinner Set

This covered vegetable dish, bowl, and gravy boat are from a complete miniature set of blue and white patterned dinnerware. Marked "Hackford;" a Staffordshire potter working around 1800, they measure approximately 1½ inches high and are valued from **$40** to **$60** each. *Courtesy of Sarah Potter Conover, Inc., New York City.*

Brass Bed

The Oriental influence on Victorian furniture is reflected in the bamboo motif apparent on this stamped brass bed, circa 1890. Possibly of French manufacture, it bears the original upholstery in perfect condition, and is a good buy at under **$175.** *Courtesy of Milne Miniatures, Robert S. Milne, New York City.*

Marble Top Desk

After a careful examination of the best, one is not so easily fooled by imitations. This Victorian Eastlake-type desk has a marble top, turned legs and stretchers, and a fine hardwood finish. The German town of Waltershausen was noted for such styling and craftsmanship, easily worth **$250** to a discerning collector. *Courtesy of Milne Miniatures, Robert S. Milne, New York City.*

Salesmen's Sample

They were quite a bit larger than ordinary miniatures but never considered as playthings. Salesmen's samples were working scale models of a salesman's wares, finely detailed and built with great care and precision in the 19th century. It's no wonder that they are treasured today. This sample walnut cylinder desk, approximately 10 inches high, sold for **$700** at auction.

Eighteenth-Century Cupboard

Serious collectors of miniature furniture are used to paying life-sized prices for rarities. But this 2½-foot, painted corner cupboard from about 1825 must have set an auction record. Even missing a piece of molding, it brought a winning bid of **$4,100**. The miniature redware pieces were sold separately at **$70** for the lot.

The Queen and Court

Richard Courtenay, a respected British manufacturer of miniatures, designed these painted metal figures, scaled at 1/32, in the 1930s. Originally $10 each, individual figures now command up to **$50.** They are, from left to right: Beefeater, Sir Francis Drake, Queen Victoria, Sir Walter Raleigh, two medieval men-at-arms. Courtenay's miniatures were transitional figures, straddling the line between toy soldiers originally made for children, and military miniatures, produced today specifically for collectors, which duplicate historic military uniforms and arms in fine detail. *All photos this page courtesy of The Soldier Shop, New York City.*

Edward the Black Prince

This miniature of medieval heroism shows Edward the Black Prince, one of the most famous commanders of the Hundred Years War, on horseback. Created by Richard Courtenay in the 1930s, it is scaled at 1/32. It originally sold for $15; today it is valued at over **$50.**

This Mounted Scots Greys Band was made by W. Britains, Ltd., at a scale of 1/32. It is difficult to determine the exact date of this miniature, but it was made sometime between 1915 and 1939. It originally cost $5.50; today it is worth **$200.**

Mounted Scots Greys Band

Costumery

A trunk of old clothes stored in the attic might have been thrown out years ago, if it hadn't been too heavy to get down the hide-away ladder. Those who wore hand-me-downs as kids keep their distance from old clothes, little realizing that in big cities around the world, antique clothing and accessories have become a booming and sophisticated business. The quintessentially American cowboy shirt (p. 169) is hunted down and bought up here by Continental shoppers, who adore the costumes of Western heroes they have come to know through American films. A $50 price tag is no object. The cultural exchange works in both directions. Americans want the 30-year-old, hand-embroidered Japanese kimonos badly enough to pay $300 (p. 168). Small stains are no deterrent in the purchasing of second-hand clothing, but wise collectors avoid signs of real deterioration.

Accessories: Styles in handbags have always reflected fashion trends. Beaded handbags, which were often made to match a wedding gown in the first half of the 19th century, cost $5 then. Now the delicate bags that have survived can bring as much as $35. And inside the bags which someone has abandoned, there are often other trifles which may turn out to be treasures — a cigarette case (p. 171), a button hook (p. 179), or some frivolity like a tiny "Pharoah" pencil (p. 176). Today, a sterling silver Art Nouveau match safe by Gorham, the prestigious Rhode Island silver factory, commands $65 (p. 172).

Jewelry: At one time, only gems and gold could give jewelry real status, but new definitions emerged in the late 19th century emphasizing artistic design and use of such materials as silver, semi-precious stones, ivory, and wood. The distinguished artists who participated in its evolution transformed "costume" jewelry into an art. René Lalique was one of the first to experiment with simpler materials, such as horn and plique á jour, a transparent enamel, working them into naturalistic Art Nouveau forms. American designers such as the Unger Brothers (p. 172) and William Kerr (p. 174) used European motifs of snakes, dragonflies, and fantastic women as the inspiration for their own designs. Simpler, more symmetrical styles came from Scotland, where jewelers studied primitive Celtic art, and from the American Arts and Crafts Movement, with its emphasis on a handmade look. Mass-produced Art Deco necklaces of chrome and plastic (p. 177) were intended to give the appearance of fine platinum and lapis. Today, this jewelry is seriously collected, and prices are rising. A search through your jewelry box for adornments you rejected long ago may turn up rewards.

Buttons: You might also find valuable buttons — decorative jewels of a different sort — inside that old jewelry box. One simple igloo button can be worth $35 or more (p. 179). A Victorian charm string, begun with the goal of assembling 1,000 buttons, was often loaded with the prettiest glass and jewel buttons of the period, and is considered a fabulous collector's find (p. 178).

Uniform and historical buttons, which commemorate military service, were decorations of a different, but even more valuable sort. Collectors, armed with metal detectors, comb old battlefields in search of rare buttons lost in the onslaughts of yesteryear. Early political buttons, made in the United States, came in sew-on form. On State occasions, marching bands paraded with such commemorative buttons sewed to their uniforms in honor of the inauguration of a new President (p. 180). Today, these are among the rarest uniform buttons known.

Suggested Reading

Albert, A. H. *Record of American and Historical Buttons,* Bicentennial edition. Hightstown, N.J., 1977.

Buck, Anne. *Victorian Costume and Costume Accesories.* Nelson, 1962.

Epstein, Diana. *Buttons.* Walker Press, 1968.

Flower, Margaret C. C. *Victorian Jewelry.* A.S. Barnes, 1973.

Gere, Charlotte. *American and European Jewelry 1830-1914.* Crown, 1975.

Luscomb, Sally C. *The Collector's Encyclopedia of Buttons.* Crown, 1967.

Rainwater, Dorothy T. *American Silver Manufacturers.* Everybodys Press, 1966.

Clothing

Kimono

Victorian Nightgown

A cascade of hand-embroidered pink blossoms spills down the back of this blue silk kimono, handmade in Japan in the late 1940s. Prices for these one-of-a-kind garments can range anywhere from **$50** to **$300** depending upon the length, fabric, and amount of handwork. Some are lined for extra warmth, as is this **$300** luxury. *All clothing courtesy of Harriet Love, New York City.*

Handmade Victorian and Edwardian white clothes — nightgowns, robes, and petticoats — were often finished with French seams and trimmed in handsome eyelet or lace. Those found in pristine condition, like this bibbed nightgown, now sell for as much as **$80.**

Velvet Coat

Cowgirl Shirt

Anyone growing up in the late 1940s remembers idealized Hollywood cowboys and cowgirls in their gleaming white outfits. But those who could attend rodeos saw the real Western kings and queens on parade — in even more dazzling attire. Those wonderful shirts have survived, to the delight of collectors from all over the world. This white rodeo shirt is appliquéd with red satin roses and would bring a boutique price of **$45-$50.**

Flea-market goers know how difficult it is to find antique velvets in good condition. They would appreciate this burgundy silk-velvet coat with its original white silk-satin lining. Details, such as the high clown collar that ties in a soft bow and the shirred low-dolman sleeves, date it at the early 1930s. While you may find one for a song, such coats bring up to **$150.**

Accessories

Beaded Handbag

This small beaded and fringed purse, with pictorial design, is probably an American work of about 1840. It is valued at **$35.** *Courtesy of Cora Ginsburg, Tarrytown, New York.*

Gentleman's Purse

This gentleman's purse is embroidered in flame stitch and is about 10 inches long. The owner's name, John Skimmer, is stitched inside. Needlework purses were popular in England until knitted and crocheted purses were introduced in the 18th century. This one dates from 1730, and is valued at **$450.** *Courtesy of Cora Ginsburg, Tarrytown, New York.*

Mesh Purse

Artful enameling makes this 6-inch metal mesh bag special. Many contemporary copies are merely painted imitations. This one is marked Mondalian Mfg. Co., a turn-of-the-century maker. Depending upon size and elaboration of detail, such bags now sell for **$20-$60.** *Courtesy of Harriet Love, New York City.*

Bags from the 1940s

Remember alligator bags? And matching shoes? Both are collectible, but more bags than shoes have survived. The bag at left is still commanding **$30-$40**. The octagonal, bronze, beaded bag, at right, has the Deco look that can bring an equally high price. *Courtesy of Harriet Love, New York City.*

Serpent Cigarette Case

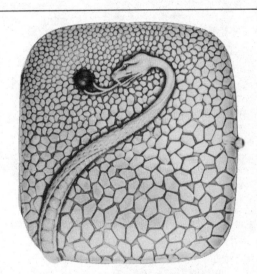

This sterling silver cigarette case is an outstanding example of the snake à la Art Deco. The wiry serpent forms a setting for the amethyst and then winds his way onto the back of the case. Made in the 1920s, it measures 3¼ inches across and has been valued at over **$165**. *Courtesy of Ilene Chaznof and Ed Pollack, Pollack Gallery, New York City.*

Fringed Fan

This elegant-looking fan is hand painted in the center, beaded on the edges, and fringed with silk. It was made during the English Regency between 1811 and 1820 to protect a lady's cheek when she sat by the fireplace on cold winter nights. Today it costs **$175** to move the air with such style. *Courtesy of Cora Ginsburg, Tarrytown, New York.*

Belt Buckles

Sterling Silver Match Safes

Seaworthy subjects in three markedly different styles comprise this group of Art Nouveau match safes. All were made in the United States between 1900 and 1910 (the one in the center by Meyers; the one at right by Gorham). Match safes like these once sold for $2.50 to $5. Today they can be bought for (from left to right) **$45**, **$55**, and **$65**.

Top: Two Art Nouveau irises meet to form this sterling silver belt buckle. It was stamped out in an imitation-repoussé technique by William Kerr around 1900. It measures 2¾ inches across and was recently sold for **$65**. Center: This Unger Bros. design in sterling silver is basically Art Nouveau design with some Egyptian influence. It was made in large and small sizes between 1903 and 1910. This rare, large size (3½ inches) is valued at **$90**. Bottom: Throughout history, lizards have inspired jewelry designers. These two harmless fellows were worked into a late-Victorian floral design. This stamped, silver-plated buckle was probably worn with a leather or grosgrain ribbon belt. To own it you would pay about **$24**. *All accessories this page courtesy of Ilene Chazanof and Ed Pollack, Pollack Gallery, New York City.*

Sterling Silver Seal

Art Nouveau was more than just graceful flowers and pretty female faces. This grotesque face on top of a seal was another typical motif. The face also inspired a popular silverware pattern of the period. Made by Unger Bros., this imitation-repoussé seal measures 2¼ inches high. It was made between 1904 and 1910 and was recently priced at **$65**.

Windmill Watch

This late-18th-century French automated watch is made of silver. The windmill turns as the watch runs, which makes this timepiece valuable. The watch was originally sold as an inexpensive novelty. It cost $125 in 1970; today it is valued at **$600.** *All watches this page courtesy of William Scolnik, Antiquarian Horologist, New York City.*

Chronograph Watch

This Waltham chronograph watch was made in the 1890s. The chronograph was developed in 1855 by E.D. Johnson for measuring time intervals, as in sporting events. It is more complex and expensive than the stop watch. This watch, set in a gold case, sold originally for about $250. Today it is valued at **$475.**

Repeating Watch

This charming repeating watch in a gold case was made in Switzerland in the 1880s. It is called a repeating watch because gongs strike and the figures move on the minutes, quarters, and hours. This watch sold originally for about $150; today, it is valued at **$4,000.**

Jewelry

Art Nouveau Brooch

This spectacular silver Art Nouveau pin was stamped out and backed with a thin sheet of silver to imitate the repoussé work. It was made in various sizes around 1900 by William B. Kerr and Co., a New Jersey manufacturer. This one, 2⅜ inches across, is the largest and rarest, and was recently valued at **$200.**

Georg Jensen Pins

Georg Jensen, a Danish sculptor, ceramicist, and silversmith, designed these sterling silver Art Deco pins in the 1930s. With the exception of the winged deer and the giant dove, these numbered designs are still being made. Approximate prices for these originals are (top): winged deer No. 81, 2⅛ inches across, **$55**; giant dove No. 70, 2⅜ inches, **$75**. Bottom: kneeling deer No. 256, 1¾ inches, **$48**; double tulip No. 100B, 1⅝ inches high, **$45**; floral with lapis lazuli No. 101, 1¾ inches, **$65.**

Snake Jewelry

The snake was one of the more ominously sensual Art Nouveau motifs. These three pieces were all American-made. Top: The 14-karat gold barrette, set with garnets, is 1⅝ inches wide and was made around 1900. It would be modestly priced at **$65.** Center: This sterling silver pin—a snake with green stone eyes—also manufactured around 1900 by Parks Brothers and Rogers in Providence, Rhode Island, measures 2¾ inches across and is valued at **$95.** Bottom: This 2-inch-wide, 14-karat gold pin, set with garnets, was made in 1875. It is valued at **$250.** *All jewelry on pages 174-177 courtesy of Ilene Chazanof and Ed Pollack, Pollack Gallery, New York City unless otherwise indicated.*

Celtic Brooch

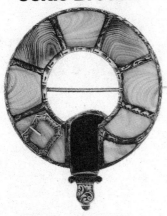

Thanks to the popularity of Sir Walter Scott, around 1880, Scottish jewelers began reinterpreting traditional national motifs. Celtic brooches, which are typically circular in design, were widely prized. This one is particularly handsome—gray agates set in chased sterling, accented with a large green bloodstone. It measures 2½ inches across and is valued at **$215**.

Stick Pins

Most of these stick pins were made in the United States between 1895 and 1915. They are shown almost full size. Some sterling silver pins, once sold for as little as $1. Those made of 14-karat gold and set with pearls cost about $5. Today, the estimates values are (top row, from left to right): gold with pearl, **$48**; sterling silver, **$15**; gold with pearl, **$35**; gold with pearl, **$32**; gold with amethyst, **$24**; (bottom row, from left to right): gold with seed pearls, **$30**; gold-washed sterling, **$45**; gold, **$38**; gold with hand-painted fish on mother-of-pearl, **$40**.

American Sterling Silver Pins

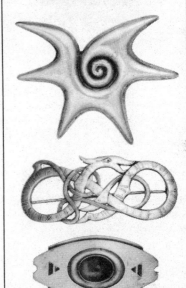

Top: This pin was made in the 1940s by Spratling, an innovative craftsman. His work is known for its heavy quality and Mexican influence — evidences of the country in which he worked. The pinwheellike pin measures 2¾ inches across and is valued at **$25**. Center: This snake pin, manufactured by Shiebler, has a curious, raised pattern of Greek and Roman numerals, a favorite device of the designer. It measures 2¾ inches across and costs about **$38**. Bottom: This pin, with an agate center, was probably handmade in a crafts school between 1876 and 1916. The clean, simple design is typical of the American Arts and Crafts movement. It measures 2⅛ inches and is valued at **$40**.

Egyptian Revival Pin

The opening of Tutankhamen's tomb in 1924 inspired many designers to work with ancient Egyptian motifs. This unusually large pin (4¾ inches wide) is a beautiful example. Made in Egypt, the pin is crafted of gilded silver, with an amethyst quartz scarab at center and yellow, royal blue, turquoise, and red enamel wings. Its current value is **$110.**

Egyptian Revival Mechanical Pencil

Made in Egypt after 1924, this tiny charmer measures only 1½ inches long when the bottom half is retracted. It is made of silver, decorated with bright blue and red enamel, and is valued at **$65.**

Dragonfly Pins

The dragonfly was a popular Art Nouveau subject. These two pins, both from around 1900, show different interpretations. At top is an American-made, sterling silver dragonfly with green glass eyes and purple glass stones on its wings. It measures 3¼ inches across and could sell for as much as **$65.** The dragonfly at bottom was hand carved out of horn. Measuring 2¼ inches wide, it could sell for as much as **$55.**

Charms

With top hat and high boots, a gentleman was properly dressed for a city stroll, and that is just the message of these painted, lead advertising charms, circa 1910. "Bullseye Boots" displayed its name on a giveaway charm; the haberdasher remains anonymous. Today, **$10** buys the hat or the single boot, in miniature form, of course. *Courtesy of Tender Buttons, New York City.*

Memorial Brooch

Wearing jewelry in memory of a deceased relative was a popular custom in Victorian England and America. Many pieces, like this 1½-inch-wide brooch, were made of gold, with glass compartments to contain a few locks of the loved one's hair. Engraved on the back of this piece are the birth and death dates of two family members who lived between 1789 and 1880. The brooch was made in the United States and is valued at approximately **$48.**

Art Deco Necklaces

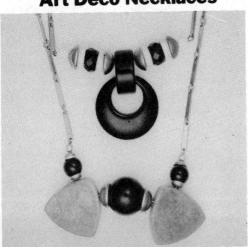

Made of bakelite and chrome, these necklaces are excellent examples of the ultra-modern design that typified the '30s in many countries. These were made in France. To buy one today, you would have to pay about **$24.**

Marcasite and Rose Quartz Necklace

Jewelry that combined sterling silver, marcasite and semiprecious stones was common in the 1930s. This necklace is unusual because rose quartz was used much less frequently than black onyx, green onyx, camelian, and chalcedony in combination with marcasite. In 1970, it was bought for $8; today it is worth **$68.**

Buttons

Charm String

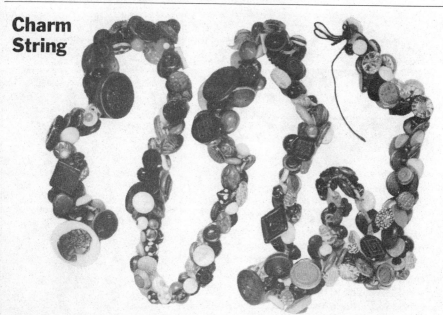

A Victorian young lady, waiting for Mr. Right, entertained herself by making a charm string. According to folklore, she would not marry until she put the 1,000th button on her string. Any charm string is worth **$100** today; but the quality of the individual buttons can raise its value considerably. *All items this and opposite page courtesy of Tender Buttons, New York City.*

Satsuma Buttons

The note which was found with these beautiful souvenirs of a trip to the West Coast tells all: "Birdie bought these in Chinatown, San Francisco, in 1905, before I was born. They are Satsuma from Japan. There should be six, but she lost one from her dress running for a trolley car with Ted in her arms — a baby." Birdie's buttons are **$30** each now.

Shibayama Studs

The Japanese laid semi-precious stones in ivory, using a technique called Shibayama, to make the delicate decoration on these round studs. The Oriental artistry contributes greatly to the **$150** value of this pair of studs.

Button Hooks

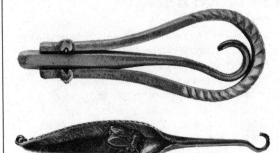

In Victorian times, selecting a hook for fastening an arm's length of glove buttons was a matter of personal taste. Not everyone would be pleased with the delicately curled, sterling silver leaf, complete with insect, shown above. Of course, when traveling, practicality outweighed personal preference, and the brass hook that folded to half its normal size was the obvious choice. The prices today, if higher, are still graduated as one would expect — the utilitarian brass hook is worth **$15**; the sterling silver leaf, **$25.**

Paperweight Button

Glass paperweights are exceedingly popular collectibles. So are paperweight buttons, made to resemble the fishbowl effect of their heavyweight counterparts. This one is valued at **$15.**

Calico Button

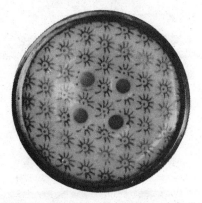

This Calico button, because it is 1 inch in diameter and set in a brass rim, is worth approximately **$50.** Printed buttons like this were made in all sizes in 1850, but it is very difficult to find such a large one.

Igloo Button

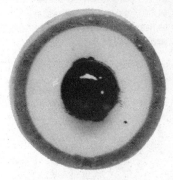

This simple china button is prized by button collectors. Once it cost a nickel; now one will bring **$35.** Measuring ½ inch, this button was made in the 1850s. It is called an igloo button because the black hump in the center, which covers the thread linking button to cloth, is shaped like an igloo.

Washington Inaugural Commemorative Button

This commemorative button, from 1789, is one of a number of patterns worn by admirers of President Washington during his administration. The border surrounding the legend "Long Live the President" represents the thirteen states. All parts of the device are impressed, except the legend, which is raised. Five years ago, this brass, one-piece button sold for **$150-$200.** Interest in the Bicentennial caused its value to soar to **$600-$750.** *Photos pages 180 and 181 courtesy of Alphaeus H. Albert, Hightstown, N.J., from Record of American Uniform and Historical Buttons.*

Constitution Era Button

At sunset on the evening of March 3, 1789, the old confederation was fired out with a 13-gun salute from the fort opposite Bowling Green in New York City; on the fourth, the new era was ushered in with the firing of an eleven-gun salute in honor of the eleven states that had adopted the Constitution. This one-piece button, commemorating that event, is made of brass, measures about 1½ inches, and is valued at **$600-$750.** A few dozen are known to exist.

Andrew Jackson Button

Twenty-four stars encircle the inscription on this button from Andrew Jackson's political campaign of 1828. Plain front, gilt buttons were the style during this period. The inscription is on the back. Today it is valued at **$200-$275** and is the sort of button that might be found in a "poke" box for **25c!**

Confederate States Army Officers Button

This gilt, two-piece button was worn on the uniform of a high-ranking officer in the Confederate States Army. It was made in Birmingham, England, by S. Buckley and Co. Almost all Confederate buttons were made by British manufacturers because the Confederates had no button factories and were forbidden to trade with the North. This button is valued at **$125-$200.**

Jeb Stuart Button

This brass button is believed to have been worn by Jeb Stuart, an officer in the Confederate States, who was famous for his hit and run tactics. It is a two-piece type and measures just under an inch. It was made in the South and its crude design contrasts sharply with those made in England. It is very rare and valued at **$400-$500.**

Continental Army Officer's Button

In 1776, this button adorned the uniform of a Continental army officer. A pewter front bears the monogram "U.S.A."; the wooden back has cords for sewing the button on a coat. The button measures a little over an inch and is very rare; there are only six or seven known in existence. It is valued at **$750-$1,000.**

Harrison-Van Buren Campaign Button

This gilt, two-piece button from the Harrison-Van Buren presidential campaign of 1840 shows a man in a stovepipe hat thumbing his nose. Two-piece buttons, with the front and back fitted together, were a popular style around 1830. This button, measuring less than an inch across, bears the mark "Scovills and Co., Waterbury." It is valued at **$250-$325.**

War of 1812 Button

This button, worn by an officer in the 32nd Regiment in the War of 1812, is the only solid-silver uniform button known. A mark on the back refers to the maker or outfitter, "Armitage, Phila." It also bears the stamp, "Best Quality." This one-piece button, measuring a little less than an inch, is valued at **$75-$125.**

Republic of Texas Navy Button

This gilt, two-piece button was worn on the uniforms of the Republic of Texas Navy, 1836-1844. Made by "G and Cie" in Paris, it is valued at **$200-$250.**

Commemoratives and Currency

World's Fairs: World's Fairs can be considered commemorative catalogs of man's inventiveness and industry. Since the first—London's Crystal Palace Exposition of 1851—souvenirs have been part and parcel of these monumental events. To this day, fairgoers find exposition halls filled with mementos seemingly made-to-order, some giveaways and others selling at minimal expense. Posters, pamphlets and pottery can always be found advertising a fair's architecture or featured innovations. In the past, fairs gave many people their first glimpses of inventions like the telephone, monorail, and the first commemorative postage stamp, all unveiled at the 1876 Centennial Exposition in Philadelphia. In 1893, the first Ferris Wheel, intended as a revolving observatory, was an astonishing engineering feat that rose 250 feet above the Columbian Exposition fairground. Some of the most valuable souvenirs have survived in the form of commemorative pottery produced especially for fairs by many distinguished manufacturers, including Lenox and Wedgwood (p. l84). But in 1939, even Fiesta Ware designer Homer Laughlin contributed to the wealth of souvenirs with his patriotic George and Martha cream pitchers (p. 185). In the summer of 1893, a lady would be grateful for a fan while touring the unair-conditioned buildings of Chicago's Columbian Exposition. Today, that fan, cherished as a valuable piece of fair ephemera (p. 184), is worth much more than the breeze it once stirred. Likewise, a 50-cent poster from the same exhibition (p. 183) might pay your way to a future expo.

Currency: Finding rare coins among your pocket change is an endlessly appealing possibility that keeps some people awake at night sorting their pennies. The odds for striking it rich via this serendipitous method are not favorable, but a few 20th-century U.S. rarities, like the double-struck cent or the 1932 quarter (p. 186) are still available for a persistent coin sleuth. But if one begins to delve into the fascinating world of currency, the rewards can be greater than any small fortune. The world's most valuable collections have been assembled with great care and scholarship over many years. Collectors specialize in hundreds of areas, each of which yields literature touching on every aspect of human life. A study of 20th-century United States coins leads one back in time to the earliest explorations of the continent, through the development of the frontier, and the gold rush. Foreign and ancient coins review the wealth, character and history of nations. In coin circles, the rarities within each specialty are always making news, particularly when valuable examples are bought and sold. Values are assigned to coins according to their condition. *Proof:* coins struck especially for collectors by mints using special dies. These coins have a shiny mirror-like surface; *Uncirculated* (Unc.): mint condition, like new; *Very Fine* (V.F.): slightly circulated; *Fine* (F): signs of wear on the edges, otherwise sharp; *Very Good* (V.G.): less than fine but with a clear impression; *Good* (G.): worn but with the date still legible. The values of all coins on pages 186 and 187 are for those in uncirculated condition as listed in *A Guide Book of United States Coins*, a reliable, annually-updated reference which also gives alternative values for the same coins in varying conditions. To have a coin appraised or evaluated, consult a reputable coin dealer, or contact one of the many collectors' clubs throughout the country. Some of these are listed on page 188.

Suggested Reading:

Coffin, Joseph. *The Complete Book of Coin Collecting*. Fifth Revised Edition, Coward, McCann & Geoghegan, Inc., 1976.

Hazelcorn, Howard. *The Complete Encyclopedia of United States Coins*. Scott Publishing Company, 1976.

Yeoman, R.S., *A Guide Book of United States Coins, 29th Edition, 1976*. Western Publishing Company, Inc.

Zimmerman, Lawrence G. "World of Fairs, 1851-1976." *Progressive Architecture*, August, 1974, pp. 64-73.

World's Fair Memorabilia

Columbian World Exposition Poster

In 1893, the World's Columbian Exposition was held in Chicago to celebrate the 400th anniversary of the landing of Columbus. Called "The White City," the fair was the site of the first Ferris Wheel, as well as a showplace for different styles of architecture. Monolithic, neoclassic structures housed exhibits of manufacturing, the arts, machinery and agriculture. This lithographed poster, 28 by 21 inches, was originally designed as a souvenir of the event and sold for about 50¢. Today, it could sell for as much as **$500**. *All photos pages 183 and 184 courtesy of Lawrence G. Zimmerman World's Fair Collection.*

Lenox Vase

This blue and white ceramic vase, made by the Lenox China Company, depicts the striking and symbolic Trylon and Perisphere, which dominated the landscape of the 1939 New York World's Fair. This 8¼-inch decorative memento, which was also made in white, cream and pale green, is worth about **$250.**

1876 Pitcher

Josiah Wedgwood first began making fine-grained stoneware in England in the 1760s. More than 100 years later, the Wedgwood firm produced this creamware commemorative pitcher for America's Centennial. One side (left) depicts Independence Hall, July 4, 1776; the other side shows Philadelphia's fair pavilion of 1876. Current estimated value of this 7½-inch pitcher is **$750.**

Souvenir Fan

This printed paper fan with wooden handle was a memento of the 1893 World's Columbian Exposition. Pictured are some of the imposing buildings built to accommodate the exhibits. The domed building on the bottom left is the Palace of Fine Arts, designed by Charles Atwood. In perfect condition, this fan would bring **$100-$200** today.

Currier & Ives Print

James Merrit Ives, partner in the 19th-century lithography firm of Currier & Ives, was also a volunteer fireman in Brooklyn, New York. His personal interest in fires accounts for many Currier & Ives prints devoted to the subject. Collectors of World's Fair memorabilia treasure this vivid, hand-colored print, which records the historic blaze that leveled the New York Crystal Palace on Tuesday, October 5, 1858. Its current estimated value is **$750.**

Exposition Advertising

This beautifully decorated envelope was issued in protest of the decision to locate the 1915 World's Panama Exposition in San Diego. New Orleans, it says, is more centrally located, and thus an obviously superior choice. The 1910 postmark indicates that plans for this exposition, and the disputes which accompanied them, were begun well in advance. To collectors of the memorabilia of world's fairs, this dramatic envelope is a **$140** item. *Courtesy of Kover King, Inc., New York City.*

Commemorative Handkerchief

This printed cotton handkerchief presents a panorama of America's early history. Pictures of the first three presidents, as well as medallions representing the thirteen original colonies, surround a representation of the Declaration of Independence. The Boston Tea Party is taking place in the bottom left corner. At the right, General Cornwallis surrenders to General Washington at Yorktown. The handkerchief, made in 1835, is worth **$650** now. *Courtesy of Cora Ginsburg, Tarrytown, New York.*

George and Martha Pitchers

For the 1939 World's Fair, Homer Laughlin, of Fiesta Ware fame, designed these 4-inch George and Martha Washington pitchers. They were sold at the American Potter Pavilion for 50¢. The patriotic couple appeals to Fiesta collectors as well as World's Fair aficionados, both of whom are willing to pay **$40** for the pair. *Courtesy of As Time Goes By, New York City.*

Coins

Penny Worth a Dollar

During the critical war year, 1943, a copper shortage forced the U.S. Treasury to issue only zinc-coated steel cents. A cent dated 1943 is today worth **70c**; 1943 D is worth **$1**; and 1943 S, **$1.75**. The mint marks appear under the date.

Mercury Dime

Though the image on this dime is commonly called Mercury, it was intended as a representation of Liberty whose wings symbolize freedom of thought. Dimes dated 1945 S (top) are worth **$13**; 1936 D (center) **$45**. Mint marks are located on the reverse at the base and to the left of the bough. But the rarest, shown at bottom, is the 1942 overstrike in which 2 is printed over 1 in the year. This coin in uncirculated condition is worth **$2,000.**

Double-Struck Cent

An improperly prepared die resulted in this common, yet famous, 1955 cent in which a completely doubled outline of date and legend are apparent. This one, worth **$450-500** in uncirculated condition, is sometimes confused with a less valuable piece that shows only minor traces of doubling.

1932 Washington Quarter

This quarter was issued to commemorate the 200th anniversary of Washington's birth. It was also the first time his image was used on a coin. The letters JF are difficult to see but appear at the base of the neck. If yours bears a D (for Denver Mint) under the wreath, as this one does, it could be worth **$475** in uncirculated condition.

Indian Head Quarter Eagle

This coin, minted from 1908 to 1929 is unique for the incursed, or stamped in, image and lettering, a departure from all previous raised-type designs. All quarter eagles of this type are worth **$150** in uncirculated condition.

Indian Head Eagle

The term *eagle* is the mint's official designation for a ten-dollar gold piece. Between 1907 and 1933, Indian Head Eagles, designed by the great French sculptor Augustus Saint-Gaudens, were struck in two varieties. The first bore no motto because President Roosevelt objected to the use of the deity's name on coins. An early 1907 eagle of this type could bring over **$6,000** in uncirculated condition. After 1908 an act of Congress restored the motto "In God We Trust" to the reverse side shown above. This 1911 coin in uncirculated condition is worth **$285**.

1872 Gold Piece

Three-dollar gold pieces were minted from 1854 to 1889, and all bear a picture of an Indian princess who has curling hair and a crown of feathers. The reverse, right, bears a wreath of tobacco, wheat, corn, and cotton. The rarest of these pieces (not shown) is dated 1854 with a small D (for Dahlonga Mint) under the wreath. It is worth **$4,000** in uncirculated condition. This 1872 example is worth **$2,800**.

Stella Gold Piece

This rare and beautiful four-dollar gold piece, named Stella, or Flowing Hair, was struck for a brief period between 1879 and 1880. Only 415 pieces were struck, and one coin, in proof condition, brings **$22,000**, while the 10 pieces of a second type (not shown), in which Stella's hair is coiled and braided, are rarer still, bringing **$90,000** each, in proof condition.

Named for its designer, George T. Morgan, this type of silver dollar (also called a Liberty Head) was minted from 1878 to 1921. His initial M is found at the truncation of the neck at the last tress. It can also be seen on the reverse, right, in the left-hand loop of the ribbon under the eagle's tailfeathers (see arrow). The rare mint mark CC beneath is for Carson City. An 1879 CC is worth **$750** in uncirculated condition; an 1889 CC, **$350**.

Morgan Silver Dollar

Collectors' Clubs and Periodicals

This list is a small sampling of hundreds of collectors' clubs and periodicals throughout the United States. Under each general classification, we have included only those organizations of broad general interest, or parent organizations for clubs with local chapters. This list has been compiled and updated with the help of collectors, dealers, and the 10th (1976) edition of the *Encyclopedia of Associations*, edited by Margaret Fisk, Gale Publishing Company.

Advertising Art

Beer Can Collectors of America
7500 Devonshire
St. Louis, Missouri 63119
Collectors interested in finding, swapping, and displaying beer cans.

Tin Container Collectors' Association
P.O. Box 4555
Denver, Colorado 80204
Collectors of antique metal containers from tobaccos, coffees, or food stuffs. Maintains library, biographical archives; compiles statistics. *Pub.:* (1) *Tin Type*, monthly; (2) Master index/directory, annual.

Banks

Mechanical Bank Collectors of America
c/o Albert Davidson
905 Manor Lane
Bayshore, New York 11706
516-666-4200
Collectors of antique mechanical banks, particularly those manufactured between 1870 and 1920. *Pub.:* (1) Journal, 3/year; (2) Member directory, annual. Formerly (1955): Mechanical Bank Collectors of Rhode Island.

Bottles

Old Bottle Magazine
Box 243
Bend, Oregon 97701
503-382-6978
Probably the most popular of the bottle magazines; a monthly.

Buttons

National Button Society of America
1132 Dunwoody Drive
Kirkwood, Missouri 63123
314-965-0711

Mrs. Carol H. Lorenz, President
Collectors and dealers of antique buttons, members of the button trade, manufacturers, libraries, and museums. Maintains library. *Pub.:* (1) *National Button Bulletin*, bimonthly; (2) Membership directory, annual; material on various types of antique buttons as well as classification booklets and a China book.

Coins

American Numismatic Association
P.O. Box 2366
Colorado Springs, Colorado 80901
303-473-9142
Membership includes individual collectors and other coin clubs. Members collect and study coins and promote the science of numismatics.

American Numismatic Society
Broadway between 155th and 156th Streets
New York, New York 10032
212-286-3030
A coin museum and a research institution which is privately funded, has an excellent library open to the public, and was founded in 1958 "to advance numismatic knowledge as relates to history, art, archeology.

Coins Magazine
Krause Publications
Ida, Wisconsin 54945
A monthly magazine. Company also publishes *Standard Catalogue of World Coins*.

Coin World
(Amos Press)
P.O. Box 150
Sidney, Ohio 45365
513-492-4141
A weekly tabloid.

Dolls

International Doll Association
10920 Indian Trail, Suite 302
Dallas, Texas 75229
214-620-1956
Jill Johnson, President
Collectors of dolls and miniatures. Purpose is the study of dolls (culture, costuming, history, makers), miniatures, and doll houses. Maintains library. Sponsors competitions, compiles statistics, bestows awards, maintains charitable program at Shriners Hospital for Crippled Children. *Pub.:* (1) *World Wide Doll News*, bimonthly; (2) *International Doll and Miniature Convention Souvenir Book*, annual. Formerly (1973): International Doll Club.

United Federation of Doll Clubs, Inc.
137 Hendricks Blvd.
Buffalo, New York 14226
716-832-6163
Mrs. Steven Orth, President
To promote educational and philanthropic work through dolls and stimulate interest in establishing children's museums with permanent doll and toy exhibits. A federation of 361 doll collectors' clubs throughout the country, and in Japan, Africa, and England. *Pub.: Doll News*, quarterly. Formerly: National Doll and Toy Collectors.

Games

Chicago Playing Card Collectors
9645 S. Leavitt Street
Chicago, Illinois 60643
Persons interested in the collecting and study of playing cards, card-trading, discussions, exhibits, films, and other activities covering the history, manufacture, and use of playing cards. *Pub.:* (1) Bulletin, bimonthly; (2) *Playing Card Mail Auctions*, quarterly; (3) Reference guides and classification listings, semiannual; (4) Membership roster, annual; prepares monthly article on playing cards for *Hobbies Magazine*, and has published a history of playing cards over 500 years.

Playing Card Collectors' Association
1511 W. Sixth Street
Racine, Wisconsin 53404
414-633-3830
Members collect and trade playing cards (single cards, decks, jokers, and spade aces). *Pub.:* Bulletin. quarterly.

Glass

International Carnival Glass Association
3142 South 35th Street
LaCrosse, Wisconsin 54601
608-788-5405
Mary Adams, Secretary

National Early American Glass Club
31 Norwood Street
Sharon, Massachusetts 02067

Depression Glass Daze
12135 North State Road
Otisville, Michigan 48463
313-631-4567
Nora Koch, Editor
This is the original national Depression glass newspaper. It is published monthly.

Metal

Pewter Collectors' Club of America
P.O. Box 239
Saugerties, New York 12477
F. Farney Eihlers, President
Collectors of pewter objects, especially pewter made in the Colonial and early Federal periods in the United States. Maintains library. *Pub.:* (1) Bulletin, semiannual; (2) Directory, biennial.

The Spooner
Route 1, Box 49
Shullsburg, Wisconsin 53586
608-965-3179
Collectors of unusual and souvenir spoons. *Pub.: The Spooner*, monthly.

Militaria

American Model Soldier and American Military Historical Society
1524 El Camino Real
San Carlos, California 94070
415-591-8125
Collectors and makers of model soldiers who are interested in books about military orders, dress, history, and prints. Includes collectors of military uniforms and paraphernalia from all periods. *Pub.: Dawk*, quarterly.

Miniatures

Miniature Figure Collectors of America
Box 311
Haverford, Pennsylvania 19041
Members of this organization collect, make, or sell miniature soldiers or figures.

National Association of Miniature Enthusiasts
P.O. Box 2621
Anaheim, California 92804
714-830-8836

Membership includes collectors and builders of miniatures, artists, writers, historians interested in miniatures. *Pub.:* (1) *Miniature Gazette*, quarterly; (2) Newsletter, irregular.

Music, Records, Musical Paraphernalia
National Sheet Music Society, Inc.
P.O. Box 2235
Pasadena, California 91105
A national organization of sheet music collectors.

United in Group Harmony Association
P.O. Box 185
Clifton, New Jersey 07011
Collectors of 1950s records.

Antique Phonograph Monthly
650 Ocean Avenue
Brooklyn, New York 11226
Allen Koenigsburg, Editor
The major publication in the field of phonograph and early record collection.

Time Barrier Express
Box 1109
White Plains, New York 10602
The leading magazine for collectors of 1950s records. Formerly: *Bim Bam Boom*.

Photographica
National Stereoscopic Association
RD 1 Box 426 A
Fremont, New Hampshire 03044
603-642-5069
Mr. Richard Russack, Director
An international organization of stereoslide and stereoview collectors. *Pub.: Stereo World*, bimonthly newsletter.

Photographic Historical Society
P.O. Box 9563
Rochester, New York 14604
Collectors of cameras and photographic materials who are interested in information, exchange, and preservation of historic photographic items.

Political Items
American Political Item Collectors
66 Golf Street
Newington, Connecticut 06111
203-666-3892
The major association of collectors of political items.

Association for the Preservation of Political Americana
P.O. Box 211
Forest Hills, New York 11375

Collectors of American political campaign memorabilia. *Pub.:* (1) Newsletter, bimonthly; (2) *The Standard*, quarterly.

National Political Button Exchange
530 Yosemite Avenue
Mountain View, California 94040
415-961-4985
Collectors of American political buttons, especially the pinback variety. Provides information on counterfeit and reproduced buttons. *Pub.:* (1) *Campaigner*, quarterly; (2) Membership roster, annual.

Political Collector
P.O. Box 164
Haddonfield, New Jersey 08033
A monthly newspaper.

Pop
Academy of Comic Art Fans and Collectors
P.O. Box 7499
North End Station
Detroit, Michigan 48202
Pub.: (1) Comic book price guide; (2) Collectors' guide: *Who's Who of American Comic Books*.

Postcards
Deltiologists of America
3709 Gradyville Road
Newtown Square, Pennsylvania 19073
215-353-1689
James L. Lowe, Director
Collectors and dealers of picture postcards, especially the earlier, antique postcards published worldwide from 1890 to 1920. Conducts mail auction sales for buying and selling of postcards. Maintains library. *Pub.:* (1) *Deltiology*, bimonthly; (2) Membership roster, annual; also publishes catalogs and guides. Formerly (1970): Better Postcard Collectors' Club.

International Postcard Collectors' Assn.
6380 Wilshire Blvd., Suite 907
Los Angeles, California 90048
Postcard collectors who promote research, maintain a library, and a collection of nearly two million postcards. *Pub.: PIC*, quarterly.

Nostalgia Collectors' Club
440 West 34th Street, 1-A
New York, New York 10001
212-868-9344
Collectors of nostalgic postcards, especially old Americana, with emphasis on early movies, radio, and transportation. Maintains library. *Pub.:* (1) *Hobbyville Herald*, quarterly;

(2) Roster of members, semiannual. Formerly: 3-D Collectors Club; (1975) Nostalgiana and 3-D Collectors Club.

Prints

Map Collectors' Circle
30 Baker Street
London, W1M 2DS, England
R.V. Tooley, Editor
Magazine, 10 issues/year

The Print Collectors' Newsletter
205 East 78th Street
New York, New York 10021
212-628-2654
An authoritative bimonthly, includes auction news and prices.

Pottery and Porcelain

National Friends of Rare Porcelain
1911 Boardwalk
Atlantic City, New Jersey 08401
609-344-1128
Mike Pred, Treasurer
Collectors of rare porcelain art and other collectible items. Grants art scholarships. *Pub.:* Newsletter, quarterly.

Railroadiana

Railroadians of America
43 Hillcrest Road
Madison, New Jersey 07940
Thomas T. Taber, Corp. Sec.
Members explore the history and present-day operation of railroads. *Pub.: Train Sheet*, quarterly; illustrated books pertaining to railroad history.

Railway and Locomotive Historical Society
c/o Edeville Railroad Museum
P.O. Box 7
South Carver, Massachusetts 02566
617-866-4526
H. Lincoln Harrison, Secretary
Persons interested in preserving documents and records of railway history. *Pub.:* (1) *Railroad History*, semiannual.

Rough and Tumble Engineers' Historical Association
Lincoln Highway
Kinzers, Pennsylvania 17535
717-442-4249
C. Daniel Brubaker, President
Retired farmers, engineers, and others interested in old gas and steam engines and farm machinery. Maintains museum of antique farm and home equipment. *Pub.: The Whistle*, 3/year.

Sports

Midwest Sports Collectors' Association
c/o Jay Barry
15261 Northfield
Oak Park, Michigan 48237
Collectors of sports items such as cards (e.g., baseball cards), yearbooks, autographs, photographs, pins, buttons, silks, guides, and registers.

Stamps

The American Philatelic Society, Inc.
Box 800
State College, Pennsylvania 16801
The largest stamp collectors' society in the U.S.

U.S. Cancellation Club
855 Cove Way
Denver, Colorado 80209
303-733-3070
Charles D. Root, Sec.-Treas.
Beginning and advanced philatelists interested in collecting postal markings and cancellations. Conducts research on postal history and markings; evaluates validity of postal items; buys and sells stamps and covers. Maintains library. *Pub.:* (1) *News*, bimonthly; (2) Roster, annual.

Linns Weekly Stamp News
(Amos Press)
Box 29
Sidney, Ohio 45236
513-492-4141
A weekly tabloid.

Stamp Show News
Box 284
Larchmont, New York 10538
914-834-3838
A monthly magazine.

Stamps
153 Waverly Place
New York, New York 10014
212-675-5407
A weekly magazine about stamp collecting. Sample copy available.

Textiles

Stevengraph Collectors' Association
Irvington-on-Hudson
New York 10533
914-591-9417
Collectors of small, colorful, woven silk pictures known as Stevengraphs, plus similarly-made bookmarkers, greeting cards, and other

products manufactured on a Jacquard loom by the firm of Thomas Stevens, Ltd., about 1861. Information exchange, reference material to museum, and other institutions provided; statistics and bibliographical material compiled.

Tools

Early American Industries Association
Division of Historical Services
Building #8
Rotterdam Industrial Park
Schenectady, New York 12306
John S. Watson, Treasurer
A national and international organization for tool collectors, dealers, and people interested in early American industries.

Early Trades and Crafts Society (E.T.C.)
60 Harvest Lane
Levittown, New York 11756
516-731-1475
Mary Jane Sayward, Membership Chairman
A regional organization for collectors of early tools. *Pub.:* a monthly information sheet about tools.

Texas Barbed Wire Collectors Association
4013 Ridgelea Drive
Austin, Texas 78331
Preserves and promotes the history of barbed wire.

Toys

International Toy Buffs' Association
425 East Green Street, Room 500 W.
Pasadena, California 91103
Collectors of children's toys. Aims to preserve old toys for children. *Pubs.:* (1) *Toy Topics*, a monthly; (2) *International Toy Directory*, a membership list published annually.

Transportation

Antique Automobile Club of America
West Derry Road
Hershey, Pennsylvania 17033
717-534-1910
The oldest automobile club in the United States and the largest automobile club in the world. *Pub.: Antique Automobile*, a bimonthly magazine.

Antique Bicycle Club of America
260 West 260th Street
Bronx, New York 10471
Dr. Roland Geist, Secretary
Collectors of bicycle and cyclana items and books. Exhibits old bicycles at shows. Maintains American Bicycle Hall of Fame and

Museum at the Richmondtown Restoration on Staten Island. *Pub.: Bicycling as a Hobby.*

The Carriage Association of America
855 Forest Avenue
Portland, Maine 04103
Members collect, restore, drive, and research horse-drawn vehicles. *Pub.:* (1) *Carriage Journal*, quarterly; (2) Membership roster, annual; reprints out-of-print items such as carriage-makers' catalogs.

Horseless Carriage Club
9031 E. Florence Avenue
Downey, California 90240
213-862-6210
Members are interested in preservation, accessories, archives, and romantic lore of old cars. *Pub.: Horseless Carriage Gazette*, bimonthly.

Antique Motor News
919 South Street
Long Beach, California
213-423-3063
A monthly magazine about antique automobiles.

Old Cars
Krause Publications
700 East State Street
Iola, Wisconsin 54945
715-445-2214
A biweekly tabloid newspaper featuring news articles about cars and a classified section. Sample copy available.

Victoriana

Victorian Society in America
Athenaeum of Philadelphia
East Washington Square
Philadelphia, Pennsylvania 19106
215-627-4252
Members interested in 19th-century arts and architecture. Aims to preserve existing outstanding examples of Victorian craftsmanship. *Pub.:* Newsletter, quarterly.

Watches and Clocks

National Association of Watch and Clock Collectors
P.O. Box 33
Columbia, Pennsylvania 17512
717-684-8261
Collectors of watches, clocks, and related items. Maintains library and museum. *Pub.:* (1) Bulletin, bimonthly; (2) *Mart*, bimonthly; (3) Roster, annual; publishes a series of monographs and horological books.